AIRCRAFT ARMAMENTS RECOGNITION

CHRISTOPHER CHANT

LONDON

IAN ALLAN LTD

Contents

Front cover:
A sequence showing the firing of an AGM-65 Maverick from a General Dynamics F-16. *General Dynamics Corp*

Back cover, top:
Sky Flash air-to-air missile firing from a Panavia Tornado. *British Aerospace*

Back cover, bottom:
A Sea Harrier firing a Sea Eagle anti-ship missile. *British Aerospace*

Sole distributors for the USA

Motorbooks International
Publishers & Wholesalers Inc
Osceola, Wisconsin 54020, USA   ®

First published 1989

ISBN 0 7110 1841 3

Published by Ian Allan Ltd, Shepperton, Surrey; and printed by Ian Allan Printing Ltd at their works at Coombelands in Runnymede, England

Introduction

One of the most evident characteristics of modern combat aircraft is the external carriage of stores at the wingtips, under the wings and under the fuselage. There are, of course, exceptions to this general tendency: the most notable are role-dedicated types such as stratetgic bombers and maritime patrol aircraft, but even these have in recent years been given provision for external stores. The reason for such a system, which became increasingly common in World War 2 and the norm for tactical aircraft in the 1950s, is simple efficiency. An internal weapon bay may offer aircraft better streamlining by removing the need for external excrescences, but it also demands a larger (and thus heavier and more expensive) airframe, and severely curtails the types and quantities of weapons that can be carried. On the other side of the coin, external carriage of stores adds considerably to drag in the loaded condition, but allows the design of a smaller (and thus lighter and less expensive) airframe fitted with hardpoints that can be configured according to weapons type as well as specific mission.

This last is a feature that pays handsome dividends over the service life of modern combat aircraft, which can today be anything up to 30 years, in comparison with perhaps five years for a type designed in the late 1930s. The process of specifying, designing, evaluating and producing modern combat aircraft is so protracted and expensive that a substantial service life is the only way to secure a reasonable return on the initial investment. Weapons can be, and are, developed far more easily and therefore swiftly, so the limitation of an airframe to a particular generation of weapon would be foolish: the need to secure a return on the larger investment (the airframe) would thereafter impose unrealistic restraints on the design of successive generations of the smaller investment (the weapons), which would have to fit into the available weapons volume.

It is standard for current tactical aircraft to carry their stores externally, therefore, with internal armament limited to cannon. (In this capacity it is worth noting that the generation of 'missile-carrier' aircraft designed in the 1950s were designed without cannon armament but then found to be sadly lacking in very short-range firepower, especially in the Vietnam War. From this time onward, therefore, one or more cannon have become standard in tactical aircraft, often supplemented by podded weapons for additional firepower in the air-to-surface role.) Apart from offering the advantages already mentioned in terms of flexibility and simple updating with newer generations of weapons as these become available, external carriage allows the limited volume available in the airframe to be used for less mutable components of the overall system: the cockpit and its associated systems, the powerplant and core fuel systems and the basic operational electronic fit. This last includes the primary sensors, the data processing and display subsystems, and the increasingly important weapon-delivery subsystem that links the weapons, sensors, pilot and flight-control system in an advanced package designed to automate and optimise the whole process of selecting the right weapon delivering it under optimum conditions to maximise the chances of scoring a hit.

The basic airframe is stressed to carry a maximum external load disposed at points optimised for weapon carriage but also to reduce the stresses on

Above:

Though very expensive, pods such as the Texas Instruments AAR-42 seen under the starboard wings of these Vought A-7E Corsair IIs offer a quantum leap in adverse-weather attack capability. The pod provides a thermal image of the terrain obliquely forward of the aeroplane, whose pilot receives the information through his Marconi raster head-up display for optimum target-recognition capability. The use of the pod reduces the number of hardpoints available for weapon carriage, but this is more than compensated by markedly improved attack accuracy. *Vought Corp*

Below:

Maximisation of any aeroplane's weapon load is made possible by the use of multiple racks such as these triple units allowing the installation of 12 500lb (227kg) Mk 82 'slick' bombs on the shoulder hardpoints of the Fairchild Republic A-10A Thunderbolt II in its battlefield close-support role.
Fairchild Industries AX10548

the airframe in level flight and also when the laden aeroplane is manoeuvred. To these hardpoints are attached pylons to support the weapons. These vary enormously in complexity and capability, ranging from the simple type designed to carry a single free-fall bomb, via more complex multiple racks, to advanced 'shoes' for missiles requiring, amongst other things, cooling of the infra-red seeker unit before launch, electrical connections for activation of various systems, and electronic connections for the priming of the missile. Some missiles also require a measure of physical separation from the launch aircraft before the motor is ignited, and in these cases there is an ejector system built into the shoe to push the missile away by pyrotechnic or, increasingly, electrical means. Such ejectors are also used on multiple racks to ensure clean separation (from the aircraft and from each other) when several stores are dropped at one time.

The single most important aspect of accurate weapon delivery is precise information about the location of the target. This can, of course, be determined in relation to the aeroplane by the pilot's eyes when he has arrived in the target area and if the conditions of light and weather are adequate. But even in perfect weather and conditions of visibility, such a process is time-consuming, and time is of the essence if the pilot is to complete the attack and depart before effective countermeasures can be implemented by the defence. Today's defensive measures can be extremely sophisticated and effective, so the pilot cannot bank on having sufficient time available to him over the target to make his eyes the primary sensor around which the mission is planned. The eyes still have an enormous part to play in finding targets of opportunity, in confirming progress dependent on other sensors, and in watching out for hostile weapons and intentions, but in modern combat operations they are definitely a secondary sensor.

Thus the primary sensors of the modern air arena are electronic. These fall into several categories of which the most important are radar, infra-red and optical. Radar is the sensor with the longest pedigree as an aircraft aid, and is today extremely capable, with the ability to search for, detect and track moving targets both above and perhaps more importantly below the aeroplane carrying the radar. The look-down capability is of particular importance in the acquisition of surface targets and opposing aircraft operating at low level; in many of the more modern equipments it allows the radar to be used for mapping, as a vital aid in accurate navigation, and for terrain avoidance, terrain clearance or terrain following. In all these latter processes the aeroplane fitted with such radar (as a mode of the main radar or as a subsidiary unit) can fly very low and very fast as a means of entering defended airspace under the enemy's ground-based radar screen: in terrain avoidance the aeroplane rolls to pass round any obstruction(s) higher than the selected flight level; in terrain clearance the aeroplane climbs just sufficiently to pass over any obstruction(s); and in terrain following the aeroplane follows the ground contour at a preselected low height. Modern radars have other roles, of course, but the above gives some indication of their basic capabilities to allow the aeroplane's approach to, and acquisition of, the target. But the great disadvantage of radar is that it is an active system. However well controlled, the fan of electromagnetic radiation beamed by the radar's transmitter is like the beam of a searchlight on a dark night, standing out strongly against the background and easily visible to anyone with 'eyes' attuned to the right wavelength. Great emphasis today is placed on passive systems that 'listen' for the emissions of active radar systems such as the standard main radar, terrain avoidance/clearance/

Above:

External carriage of weapons helps to diversify the weapon types that can be carried by any particular aeroplane type. This is a General Dynamics F-16 Fighting Falcon, which was developed as a lightweight air-combat fighter, but soon evolved into a genuine multi-role type with a wide assortment of weapons. Seen here are 20mm ammunition for the M61A1 Vulcan cannon, an ALQ-131 electronic countermeasures pod (centre front) with the white-painted B61 and B43 tactical nuclear weapons plus a drop tank behind it, and in the angled-back lateral rows 'Snakeye' retarded and 'slick' free-fall bombs, various types of cluster and dispenser weapons, two rocket-launcher pods, two triplets of AGM-65 Maverick air-to-surface missiles, two 'Paveway' series laser-guided bombs, and on the aeroplane four AIM-9 Sidewinder air-to-air missiles. *General Dynamics 30-73568*

following radar, radar altimeter and Doppler navigation radar, and for optional features such as active jammer pods or rear-warning radar. Passive systems are carried by most tactical aircraft for two basic functions: to warn crews when their aircraft are being illuminated by hostile radars, so allowing countermeasures to be implemented, and to provide a combination of target identification, range and bearing data for the launch of a passive-homing anti-radar missile.

So while active radar offers great capability, it can also betray the operator. For this reason, therefore, there is increasing emphasis on two types of passive sensor to supplement (but certainly not to replace) radar. These two types are based on heat and light. The heat sensor is based on the gathering and analysis of infra-red radiation by a sensor that is cooled to increase the differential between itself and the objects at which it looks. This allows the sensor to 'see' minute variations in temperature, allowing the creation of a thermal image with precision and discrimination almost equal to that of a purely optical system. The main application of infra-red (IR) sensors in tactical aircraft is for navigation and target-acquisition at night and under adverse weather conditions, the Forward-Looking Infra-Red (FLIR) sensor generally being accommodated in a mounting that can be elevated and/or traversed under crew control to look in any desired direction, or under computer control to remain fixed, with limits, on a specific area of interest regardless of aircraft attitude and manoeuvring. The optical sensor is generally a low-light-level TV, in which extremely low levels of light can be used in an electronically-enhanced electro-optical (EO) system to provide a conventional image of the outside world even at night and under adverse weather conditions. Like the FLIR system, such an EO system is usually accommodated in a trainable mounting. Some aircraft have these mountings as part of the basic sensor fit, good examples being the Grumman A-6E/TRAM, which has a FLIR as part of its undernose Hughes AAS-33 Target Recognition and Attack Multi-sensor turret, and the McDonnell Douglas F-4E, of which many are fitted in the port wing with the Northrop ASX-1 Target Identification System, Electro-Optical. But such systems are extremely expensive, and it is increasingly common to find them as podded items that can be installed on relevant aircraft as required. A particularly good example of the type is the Martin Marietta LANTIRN (Low-Altitude Navigation and Targeting Infra-Red for Night) system, a highly capable equipment with a navigation pod containing a FLIR and terrain-following radar, and an attack pod containing a FLIR and laser ranger/designator.

Data from these sensor systems can be presented to the crew in several forms, most notably on the HDD (Head-Down Display) and HUD (Head-Up Display). The HDD is a cathode-ray tube display in the cockpit, with overlaid symbology called up as required by the operator, while the HUD is an optical panel in front of the pilot's eyes, allowing him to look ahead and still be provided with basic flight and weapon-aiming information (pictorial and symbolic) focused at infinity so that he need not refocus his eyes to assimilate the information. This is one of the fastest-developing fields in military aviation, offering enormous leaps in capability by using computers to filter information and feed the pilot or crew with only the data relevant to the task in hand and keeping additional data stored until specifically requested. This also allows the HUD to be used as the pilot's main weapon-aiming sight, his view of the target being complemented by all the relevant factors of aircraft attitude, speed and height plus weapons availability and launch parameters. Modern cockpits are increasingly of the HOTAS (Hands On Throttle And Stick) variety, and the presentation of aiming symbology in the HUD accords well with such a control philosophy in leaving the pilot free to concentrate his attentions on the tactical situation without having to drop and refocus his eyes on cockpit screens or dials, or to move his hands to find weapon firing buttons or switches.

Closely allied to this technology is that for air-to-surface weapon guidance. FLIR and/or EO information can be used to prime a missile about its target. The relevant thermal or optical image is locked into the missile's guidance system, or even updated in flight (via a data-link pod such as the Hughes AXQ-14), the weapon comparing the stored and actual image to secure an accurate impact: typical of such a weapon is the British AJ168 version of the Anglo-French Martel (TV guidance) and the American GBU-15 EO-guided glide bomb. An alternative system uses laser (coherent light) energy. This can be used to provide extremely accurate range data, and also to 'paint' the desired target with the energy whose reflection is the homing source for laser-guided weapons such as some variants of the Hughes AGM-65 Maverick missile and the increasing number of laser-homing bombs such as the French Matra LGB, the Israeli IAI Opher and the US Texas Instruments 'Paveway' series, which can also home on to energy bounced off the target by a third-party laser of the right frequency. Radar has only modest applications in the overland air-to-surface role, active radar being technically unsuited and moreover too expensive, and passive radar being reserved for attacks on hostile emitters in weapons such as the French Matra ARMAT and the US Texas Instruments AGM-88 HARM. But radar homing is well suited to anti-ship and air-to-air use. With notable exceptions such as the IR-homing Kongsberg Penguin from Norway, anti-ship missiles are generally of the active or semi-active radar homing varieties. Both types cruise towards their targets under control of an autopilot, only in the immediate vicinity of the target activating their terminal homing systems. Active radar is well suited to the long-range missile, and semi-active radar to the short and medium-range type whose target can be 'painted' with radar energy by the missile's launch platform or, rarely, by a third party. Active and semi-active radar homing is used in a number of air-to-air missiles, typically the Hughes AIM-54 Phoenix (active radar) and Raytheon AIM-7 Sparrow (semi-active radar). However, semi-active radar has the severe tactical disadvantage of forcing the launch aircraft to fly on towards the target and illuminate it with radar energy, until the missile impacts. This has placed greater emphasis on high-performance missiles of modest size carrying active radar (such as the French Matra MICA and US Hughes AIM-120 AMRAAM), and on passive homing missiles such as the classic US Ford AIM-9 Sidewinder with IR homing. After launching active radar or passive IR missiles the launch aircraft can break away towards safety.

1: Barrelled Weapons

GIAT DEFA 553

Type: aircraft cannon
Calibre: 30mm
Overall dimensions: length 1.66m (65.35in)
Weight: complete weapon 85.0kg (187.4lb), or 160kg (352.7lb) with
    feed mechanism and empty magazine
Muzzle velocity: between 765 and 820m (2,510 and 2,690ft)/sec
    depending on ammunition type
Rate of fire: 1,300 rounds/min

This important series of French aircraft cannon was originated with the
DEFA 551, and entered production in 1954 as the **DEFA 552** for high-altitude
fighters. The design is modelled closely on German revolver developments
in World War 2, most notably the Mauser MG213C, and thus has many
similarities to the British Aden, which was developed at much the same time
from the same conceptual sources. The weight of the complete weapon is
80kg (176.4lb) and the rate of fire 1,250 rounds/min.

The **DEFA 552A** is a development of the DEFA 552 with features of the
DEFA 553 such as a chromed barrel. This increases weight to 81kg (178.5lb),
but boosts the rate of fire to 1,300 rounds/min and increases barrel life to
5,000 rounds.

The **DEFA 553** is in essence a product improved DEFA 552 whose
development was initiated in 1968 for production from 1971. The areas in
which improvement was sought were electro-mechanical reliability and ease
of operation, and installation was also facilitated by provision of a feed
mechanism able to accept linked ammunition from either side without
modification. The adoption of a nitro-chrome steel barrel reduces barrel wear
and so increases life to 4,000 rounds, and a pressure-reducing fitting can be
installed at the muzzle to reduce the problem of propellant gas ingestion
when the muzzle is close to an inlet. The type has provision for continuous
fire, or for 0.5sec or 1.0sec bursts.

The **Dassault-Breguet CC 420** is the main podded installation of the
DEFA 552, 552A, 553 or 554 cannon types for carriage on underfuselage or
underwing installations. The pod comes in two basic configurations, namely
the **CC 420 Type A** with a double-ended (closed-loop) feed system for 180
rounds, and the **CC 420 Type B** with a single-ended (case-ejecting) system
for 250 rounds. Development of the pod began in 1970, and in 1978 the
system was put into production to meet French and export orders. The
loaded weights of the Type A and Type B pods are 300 and 325kg (661.4 and
716.5lb) respectively.

Above:
The Fiat G91 light attack aircraft was developed with a quartet of 0.5in (12.7mm) Browning M3 machine guns in pairs on the sides of the forward fuselage. This is the G91R/3 reconnaissance model with a pair of 30mm DEFA 552 cannon each with 125 rounds.
Hunting Engineering Ltd

GIAT DEFA 554

Type: aircraft cannon
Calibre: 30mm
Overall dimensions: length 2.01m (79.13in)
Weight: complete weapon about 85.0kg (187.4lb), or 160kg (352.7lb)
  with feed mechanism and empty magazine
Muzzle velocity: between 765 and 820m (2,510 and 2,690ft)/sec
  depending on ammunition type
Rate of fire: 1,200 or 1,800 rounds/min

The **GIAT DEFA 554** is a considerable development of the basic DEFA 552 and DEFA 553 theme, with greater reliability and much improved rate of fire. The latter has been obtained by better use of the five-chamber revolver cylinder, in which three rather than two chambers are used for the loading process. This boosts the firing rate considerably without the need for any increase in the speed of the action's operation, and the weapon has thus been fitted with an electronic control unit to provide rates of 1,200 rounds/min for the ground-attack role, and 1,800 rounds/min for the air-to-air role.

Below:
The latest version of French standard 30mm aircraft cannon is the DEFA 554.
IMP Publishing Services (IMPPS)

Above:

Developed jointly by Aeritalia and EMBRAER, the AMX light attack aeroplane is being produced with two types of fixed armament: the Italian version has a single 20mm M61A1 Vulcan cannon in the port side of the nose with 350 rounds, and the Brazilian version illustrated has two 30mm DEFA 554 cannon each with 125 rounds. *EMBRAER 2CA13B4*

MAUSER BK 27

Type: aircraft cannon
Calibre: 27mm
Overall dimensions: length 2.31m (7.58ft); width 0.296m (11.65in);
  height 0.246m (9.69in)
Weight: complete weapon 100kg (220.5lb)
Muzzle velocity: 1,025m (3,363ft)/sec
Rate of fire: selectable 1,700 or 1,000 rounds/min

The **Mauser BK 27** is a powerful dual-role (air-to-air and air-to-surface)
cannon currently installed in a pod under the Dassault-Breguet/Dornier Alpha
Jet A, and internally in the Panavia Tornado and Saab-Scania JAS39 Gripen.
Among the notable features of the weapon are its high rate of fire and high
muzzle velocity, and the ballistically-matched projectiles of various types are
fitted with a fuse system that operates effectively at high angles of impact.

Below:
**The 27mm Mauser BK27 cannon was developed specifically for the Panavia
Tornado multi-role aircraft, which carries two of these powerful weapons
(each with 360 rounds) in the forward fuselage, their muzzle ports being
visible on the lower part of the nose in front of the windscreen.** *Panavia*

OERLIKON-BÜHRLE KCA

Type: aircraft cannon
Calibre: 30mm
Overall dimensions: length 2.691m (8.83ft); width 0.2425m (9.5in); height 0.2495m (9.82in)
Weight: complete weapon 136kg (299.8lb)
Muzzle velocity: 1,030m (3,379ft)/sec
Rate of fire: 1,350 rounds/min

The **Oerlikon-Bührle KCA** is one of the world's most powerful air-to-air cannon, and is intended for internal and podded installations. The weapon is used currently only on the JA37 interceptor version of the Saab Viggen, and is characterised by high muzzle energy to provide a 1,000m (1,094yd) flight time of 1.139sec and a very flat trajectory.

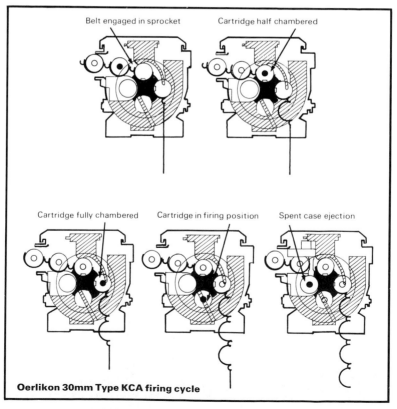

Oerlikon 30mm Type KCA firing cycle

The 30mm Oerlikon-Bührle KCA is one of the most potent of modern aircraft cannon, firing a heavy projectile with an exceptionally high muzzle velocity for high kinetic energy and short flight-time over a flat trajectory.
Oerlikon-Bührle 61793

A side view of the JA37 reveals the massive fixed but external installation of the Oerlikon-Bührle KCA under the Viggen's fuselage. In the centre of the installation is the cover that hinges down at the rear to provide access to the breech and 150-round magazine. *Saab-Scania/A. Anderson*

ROYAL SMALL ARMS FACTORY ADEN
Mk 4

Type: aircraft cannon
Calibre: 30mm
Overall dimensions: length 62.6in (1.59m); width 9.45in (0.24m);
  height 9.69in (0.246m)
Weight: complete weapon 192lb (87.1kg)
Muzzle velocity: 2,430ft (741m)/sec
Rate of fire: 1,200 to 1,400 rounds/min

Like the DEFA series of 30mm aircraft cannon, the **RSAF Aden Mk 4** has its
origins in the German Mauser MG 213C revolver cannon of World War 2, and
though developed in the late 1940s it is still a powerful weapon in the
air-to-air and air-to-surface roles. The type is used in a large number of fixed
two- and four-cannon installations, and can also be fitted in the French
Matra SA 10 pod and the Swedish **FFV Aden** pod, which uses the cannon
variant designation **M/55** in Swedish service. The FFV pod's empty and
loaded weights are 290 and 354kg (639.3 and 802.5lb) respectively; the
standard ammunition capacity is 150 rounds, though there is an option for
200 rounds.

The **Aden Mk 5 (Straden)** is an improved version designed for greater
reliability and rate of fire increased to 1,500/1,700 rounds/min. Development
has not resulted in production Aden Mk 5 cannon, for several of the weapon's
best features have been used in the more modern Aden 25 cannon.

Below:
**It is now fairly common practice to use advanced trainers in the weapons
training and light attack role, the disposable armament being complemented
by a podded cannon. This is a BAe Hawk T Mk 1 with an 800lb (363kg) ventral
pack containing one 30mm Aden Mk 4 cannon, and sporting two AIM-9L
Sidewinders under the wings.** *John Dunnell*

ROYAL SMALL ARMS FACTORY ADEN 25

Type: aircraft cannon
Calibre: 25mm
Overall dimensions: length 90.0in (2.286m); width 9.45in (0.24m);
    height 9.69in (0.246m)
Weight: complete weapon 203lb (92.0kg)
Muzzle velocity: 3,445ft (1,050m)/sec
Rate of fire: 1,650 to 1,850 rounds/min

The new **RSAF Aden 25** is based on the Aden Mk 5 series, but fires the new range of NATO 25mm ammunition at much higher rates of fire than its predecessor. The result is a three-fold increase in killing power, yet the weapon can still be installed in mountings designed for the earlier Aden cannon as it is dimensionally identical but has almost one-third less recoil force. The initial application of the Aden 25 is in the BAe Harrier GR Mk 5, which has two such cannon in podded installations scabbed on to the underside of the fuselage: each pod contains one Aden 25 and 100 rounds of ammunition, and the two pods together weigh 948lb (430kg).

Below.
First used in the BAe Harrier GR Mk 5 (the British version of the McDonnell Douglas AV-8B Harrier II developed in the USA for the US Marine Corps) is the RSAF Aden 25, a new 25mm cannon both lighter and harder-hitting that its 30mm predecessor. As in the earlier Harrier variants the cannon are located in the underfuselage strakes of the Lift-Improvement Device. *BAe 8601088*

GENERAL ELECTRIC GAU-2B/A MINIGUN

Type: aircraft six-barrel externally-powered 'Gatling' machine gun
Calibre: 7.62mm (0.3in)
Overall dimensions: length 31.56in (0.802m) with motor; width 10.5in (0.267m); height 7.87in (0.2m)
Weight: complete weapon 56.5lb (25.6kg) with motor
Muzzle velocity: 2,750ft (838m)/sec
Rate of fire: variable up to 4,000 or 6,000 rounds/min (*see below*)

The **General Electric GAU-2B/A Minigun** is a light but very useful machine gun developed on the conceptual basis of the M61 Vulcan aircraft cannon, and uses the General Electric 'Gatling' principle to secure very high rates of fire combined with great reliability. The system is based on an externally-powered barrel assembly rotating round a common axis, each of the six barrels having its own bolt assembly operated by a cam follower which, riding in a cam path machined into the rotor assembly, converts the rotor's circular movement into the bolt's fore-and-aft movement for the cycle of chambering, firing and extracting one round per barrel per complete rotation. Thus, even at the Minigun's maximum rate of 6,000 rounds/min, each barrel fires only 1,000 rounds. The weapon is offered with a choice between two motors, one offering a maximum rate of 6,000 rounds and the other of 4,000 rounds/min, though rates as low as 300 rounds/min are also possible. The designation GAU-2B/A is used for the basic US Air Force weapon, the equivalent designation for the US Army version, which generally has the 4,000 round/min rate, being **M134 Minigun**. The Minigun can be used in a number of pintle-mounted or turreted installations, mostly on helicopters and light tactical aircraft, and is also offered in a pod (designated **SUU-11B/A** by the US Air Force and **M18E1** by the US Army) that weighs 324lb (147.0kg) complete with 1,500 rounds of ammunition.

Right:
The A-37B Dragonfly is the dedicated attack derivative of the Cessna T-37 trainer, and its fixed armament comprises a nose-mounted General Electric GAU-2B/A Minigun with 1,500 rounds of 7.62mm (0.3in) ammunition. The muzzle port for this 'Gatling' type machine gun is located on the port side of the upper nose, just to the rear and right of the inflight-refuelling probe.
Cessna

19

GENERAL ELECTRIC GAU-8/A AVENGER

Type: aircraft externally-powered 'Gatling' seven-barrel cannon
Calibre: 30mm
Overall dimensions: length 114.0in (2.896m); diameter 14.0in (0.356m)
Weight: complete weapon 620 lb (281.2kg)
Muzzle velocity: 3,240ft (988m)/sec with API, and between 3,400 and 3,450ft (1,036 and 1,052m)/sec with HEI and TP ammunition
Rate of fire: selectable 2,100 rounds/min with one motor, or 4,200 rounds/min with two motors

The **General Electric GAU-8/A Avenger** is the world's most devastating aircraft gun by a very considerable margin, and was designed specifically to arm the Fairchild Republic A-10A Thunderbolt II. The A-10A is a dedicated tank-killing aircraft, and its gun plus associated ammunition reflect the fact, the API round being built round a depleted uranium penetrator. The heavy projectile has high velocity and this translates into greater projectile accuracy and, given the mass of the projectile, enormous kinetic energy at the target. The gun generates great heat when firing, and with the standard quantity of ammunition the GAU-8/A is designed to fire 10 2sec bursts each separated by a 1min cooling period. Weight is obviously great with so massive a cannon and associated equipment, but a saving of 600lb (272.2kg) was made by choosing aluminium rather than steel for the ammunition cases. The magazine is a cylindrical unit located immediately behind the cannon, and can contain 1,350 rounds, though the standard loading is 1,174 rounds. The total weight of the system with maximum ammunition is 4,029lb (1,828kg). The complete length of the system is 238.5in (6.058m) and its height is 39.75in (1.01m).

GENERAL ELECTRIC GAU-12/U EQUALISER

Type: aircraft externally-powered 'Gatling' five-barrel cannon
Calibre: 25mm
Overall dimensions: length 83.2in (2.113m); diameter 11.0in (0.279m)
Weight: complete weapon 270lb (122.5kg)
Muzzle velocity: 3,280ft (1,000m)/sec for API, and 3,400ft (1,036m)/sec for HEI and TP ammunition
Rate of fire: normally 3,600 rounds/min, with 4,200 rounds/min possible

The **General Electric GAU-12/U Equaliser** is the first of the General
Electric 'Gatling' weapons to make use of the new NATO standard 25mm
ammunition also used by the British Aden 25. The weapon is derived
technically from the GAU-8/A. The first application of the weapon is as the
armament of the McDonnell Douglas AV-8B Harrier II close-support aircraft,

which has the system incorporated into the two pods attached to the underside of the fuselage and thus forming part of its lift-improvement system. The left-hand pod contains the GAU-12/U together with its pneumatic drive, whilst the right-hand pod accommodates 300 rounds of ammunition fed to the cannon through a bridge structure connecting the two pods towards their after ends. The weight of the complete system is 900lb (408kg) empty and 1,230lb (558kg) loaded.

USA

GENERAL ELECTRIC GAU-13/A

Type: aircraft externally-powered 'Gatling' four-barrel cannon
Calibre: 30mm
Overall dimensions: length 110.0in (2.794m); diameter 12.0in (0.305m)
Weight: complete weapon 339lb (153.8kg)
Muzzle velocity: 3,240ft (988m)/sec with API, and 3,400ft (1,036m)/sec
    with HEI and TP ammunition
Rate of fire: normally 2,400 rounds/min

The **General Electric GAU-13/A** is a lightweight version of the GAU-8/A Avenger with four rather than seven barrels. The weapon uses the same ammunition and reverse-clearing system as the GAU-8/A, the latter ensuring that live rounds are extracted from the hot breeches when the trigger is released, thereby removing the possibility of 'cook-off' firing. The sole application of the cannon is in the **GPU-5/A** pod, also known as the **GEPOD 30**. This accommodates 353 rounds of ammunition, and weighs 1,909lb (865kg) loaded.

USA

GENERAL ELECTRIC GECAL 50

Type: aircraft externally-powered 'Gatling' three-barrel machine gun
Calibre: 0.5in (12.7mm)
Overall dimensions: length 46.5in (1.181m); diameter 8.0in (0.203m)
Weight: complete weapon 68lb (30.85kg)
Muzzle velocity: 2,900ft (884m)/sec
Rate of fire: up to 4,000 rounds/min with linkless feed mechanism

The **General Electric GECAL 50** is another of the company's family of 'Gatling' weapons, in this instance an extremely powerful machine gun designed to use the whole range of ammunition types developed for the classic M2/M3 series of heavy machine guns. The basic three-barrel version is fitted with a controlled-burst device for salvoes of 10 rounds which, fired at the rate of 4,000 rounds/min, arrive on the target almost simultaneously for maximum destructive effect. A six-barrel version has also been developed, and this has a firing rate of 8,000 rounds/min at a weight of 96lb (43.6kg).

GENERAL ELECTRIC M61A1 VULCAN

Type: aircraft externally-powered 'Gatling' six-barrel cannon
Calibre: 20mm
Overall dimensions: length 73.8in (1.875m); diameter 13.5in (0.343m)
Weight: complete weapon 265lb (120.2kg)
Muzzle velocity: 3,400ft (1,036m)/sec
Rate of fire: variable up to 6,600 rounds/min

The **General Electric M61A1 Vulcan** is the most widely used aircraft cannon of the Western world, and was the first member of the General Electric 'Gatling' family of externally-powered rotary-action weapons. The M61A1 current variant dates from 1956, when General Electric realised that the problems it was encountering with the development of rotary-action cannon using linked feed systems were basically insuperable at the firing rates being attained, and therefore turned to a linkless feed arrangement with a drum magazine. The first installation of the Vulcan was on the Lockheed F-104 Starfighter interceptor, and trials soon confirmed that a single weapon of this type offered many advantages over the alternative of a multiple battery of guns. The Vulcan has thus become the primary fixed armament of US fighters designed from the mid-1950s onwards, the size of the weapon and its feed system and ammunition magazine dictating the design of individual installations for each type. The type is also available in a self-powered form with the US Air Force designation **GAU-4**.
   Apart from its internal installations, the Vulcan can also be fitted in a pod, the two standard types being the **SUU-16/A** with a M61A1 using external ram-air power supply, and the **SUU-23/A** with the self-powered GAU-4 cannon. The SUU-16/A weighs 1,615lb (733kg) loaded, and is used by the US Army with the designation **M12**. The SUU-23/A weighs 1,720lb (780kg), and is used by the US Army with the designation **M25**.

Below:
An SUU-23/A 20mm cannon pod on the centreline hardpoint of a McDonnell Douglas Phantom FRG Mk 2 of No 19 Squadron at RAF Akrotiri in Cyprus.
Denis J. Calvert

GENERAL ELECTRIC M197

Type: aircraft externally-powered 'Gatling' three-barrel cannon
Calibre: 20mm
Overall dimensions: length 71.93in (1.827m); diameter 10.8in (0.267m)
Weight: complete weapon 145lb (65.8kg) with drive motor
Muzzle velocity: 3,380ft (1,030m)/sec
Rate of fire: selectable between 750 and 3,000 rounds/min

The **General Electric M197** is essentially a version of the M61 Vulcan series with only three (but longer) barrels and optimised for use in helicopter and light fixed-wing aircraft installations, in trainable turrets and pintle installations. The standard podded installation is the **GPU-2/A**, which is often called the **Lightweight Gun Pod**. The pod was designed for use by helicopters and a wide variety of tactical aircraft, and has a capacity of 300 rounds. The pod's loaded weight is 585.9lb (266kg).

Below.
The General Electric M197 is essentially a three-barrel derivative of the M61A1 in the same 20mm calibre, but intended primarily for turreted installation in attack helicopters such as the Bell AH-1W SuperCobra with about 750 rounds of ammunition. The M197 can be seen here under the long instrumentation probe below the nose of this prototype helicopter, which also carries a quadruple BGM-71 TOW anti-tank missile installation under its starboard stub wing. *Bell Textron 026286*

USA

McDONNELL DOUGLAS HELICOPTERS M230

Type: aircraft externally-powered single-barrel cannon
Calibre: 30mm
Overall dimensions: length 74.4in (1.889m) including muzzle brake;
   width 10.0in (0.254m); height 11.5in (0.292m)
Weight: complete weapon 123lb (55.8kg)
Muzzle velocity: 2,600ft (792m)/sec
Rate of fire: variable up to 750 rounds/min

The **McDonnell Douglas Helicopters M230** is a very powerful
single-barrel cannon developed in parallel with the General Electric M188 in a
competitive programme designed to provide the barrelled armament for the
US Army's Advanced Attack Helicopter, a competition eventually won by the
Hughes AH-64. The M230 was the first cannon to make use of the excellent
Hughes-developed 'Chain Gun' operating principle for positive external
control of all phases of the loading, firing and clearing cycle.

Below:
**For the fire suppression of local weapons the McDonnell Douglas Helicopters
AH-64A Apache battlefield helicopter carries an underfuselage McDonnell
Douglas Helicopters M230 cannon fed by a closed-loop system with 30mm
ammunition from a 1,200-round fuselage magazine. On the underwing
hardpoints are eight AGM-114A Hellfire air-to-surface missiles and two
18 tube pods for 2.75in (69.86mm) unguided rockets.** *Denis J. Calvert*

2: Air-to-Air Missiles

FRANCE

MATRA R530

Type: medium range air-to-air missile
Dimensions: diameter 0.263m (10.35in); length 3.294m (129.29in) for
semi-active radar homing version and 3.198m (125.9in) for infra-red
homing version; span 1.103m (43.4in)
Weight: total round 192kg (423.3lb) for semi-active radar version and
193.5kg (426.6lb) for infra-red homing version
Warhead: 27kg (59.5lb) pre-fragmented or continuous-rod blast
fragmentation
Powerplant: (early production models) one Hotchkiss-Brandt/SNPE
Antoinette dual-thrust solid-propellant rocket, or (later production
models) one SNPE Madeleine dual-thrust solid propellant rocket
Performance: speed Mach 2.7; range 18,000m (19,685yd)
Guidance: EMD AD26 semi-active radar homing or SAT AD3501
infra-red homing

Introduced in the early 1960s as armament for the Dassault Mirage III and
later used on the Dassault-Breguet Mirage F1 and Vought F-8E(FN) Crusader,
the **Matra R530** was developed from 1957 as a major air-to-air weapon with
a large body, fixed delta wings and small tail-mounted control surfaces
indexed in line with the wings. The basic airframe/powerplant combination
was produced with alternative semi-active radar and IR seekers, neither of
which has proved particularly successful. The seeker units are
interchangeable at squadron level, and the standard operating practice with
the R530 is similar to that used with most Soviet air-to-air missiles: fighters
generally carry a pair of missiles with different homing heads to provide a
fully maximised interception capability under all conditions. The IR seeker is
claimed to be of the all-aspect type, but is in fact limited to rear-hemisphere
engagements in all but the most advantageous conditions. Though of only
very modest capability, the R530 had little commercial competition and sold
to the air forces of 14 countries operating the French fighters fitted with the
Cyrano Ibis, II and IV radars to which the semi-active radar-homing R530
version is matched. The Aéronavale used a slightly modified version of the
AD26 seeker matched to the Magnavox APQ-94 radar of its Crusader fighters.

Right:
**The Dassault-Breguet Mirage F1 is a genuine multi-role fighter, as indicated by
this armament layout. From front to rear the weapons are two 30mm DEFA 553
cannon, two Matra R530 medium range air-to-air missiles, two podded 30mm
DEFA cannon, two Matra R550 Magic short-range air-to-air missiles, free-fall
bombs of various sizes, eight BAP 100/BAT 120 anti-runway/anti-vehicle**

bombs, eight Durandal anti-runway bombs flanking an AS30 air-to-surface missile, six Belouga cluster bombs flanking a 1,700l (347Imp gal) drop tank, 68 and 100mm (2.68 and 3.94in) Thomson Brandt TBA-68 and TBA-100 unguided rockets complete with their launchers, and Matra F1 36-tube rocket launchers flanking a drop tank. *Dassault-Breguet*

MATRA SUPER 530F

Type: medium/long range air-to-air missile
Dimensions: diameter 0.263m (10.35in); length 3.54m (139.37in); span
  0.64m (25.2in) forward and 0.90m (35.43in) aft
Weight: total round 250kg (551.1lb)
Warhead: 30kg (66.1lb) Thomson Brandt blast fragmentation
Powerplant: one Thomson Brandt/SNPE Angèle dual-thrust solid
  propellant rocket
Performance: speed Mach 4.6; range 35km (21.75 miles)
Guidance: EMD Super AD26 semi-active radar homing

Developed from the early 1970s as armament for the Dassault-Breguet
Mirage F1 fighter, the **Matra Super 530F** high-speed missile is based
loosely on the aerodynamics of the R530 modified to a configuration similar
to that of the American RIM-66/RIM-67 Standard series of surface-to-air
missiles. It is characterised by cruciform wings of very low aspect ratio
(spanning about 0.50m/19.7in), trailed by a cruciform of slightly greater-span
control surfaces indexed in line with the wings and located at the very tail of
the missile. Internally the Super 530 is completely different from its
predecessor, being a new and advanced weapon matched to the Cyrano IV
radar. The missile has twice the range and target-acquisition capabilities of
the R530, as well as snap-up capability against aircraft 9,000m (29,530ft)
higher than the launch aircraft; the type also possesses a useful snap-down
capability in the order of 7,000m (22,965ft). The Super 530F began to enter
service in 1979 after an eight-year development period, and has been
produced in substantial numbers for Mirage F1 aircraft in French and export
service. The weapon can also be used by Dassault-Breguet Mirage 2000C
fighters fitted with the RDM radar.

The **Super 530D** is a development of the Super 530F with so many
technical improvements in significant features as to be virtually a new
weapon based on digital processing, a new homing head working in the
more accurate and less jammable Doppler fashion, and increased rocket
power. The Super 530D is matched specifically to the RDI and RDM
pulse-Doppler radars of the Dassault-Breguet Mirage 2000 series. This
version of the missile has a weight of about 265kg (584.2lb) and a length of
3.80m (149.61in), uses an improved motor for a speed of Mach 4.6+ and a
range of up to 60km (37.3 miles), and has better snap-down capability than
the Super 530F. The missile can deal with Mach 3 targets at a height of
24,000m (78,740ft) and, considerably more importantly, with targets flying
fast and low in ground clutter conditions. Thus the Super 530D can fairly be
claimed as the only Western missile of non-American origins to match, at
least in part, the capabilities of the AIM-54 Phoenix as a weapon suitable for
operations at all altitudes, at all aspects and in all weathers. Apart from
France, the missile has been bought by Mirage 2000 export customers such
as Egypt, Greece and India.

Above:
A Dassault-Breguet Mirage 2000 launches one of its two Matra Super 530 air-to-air missiles. *Engins Matra*

MATRA R550 MAGIC 1

> *Type:* short range dogfighting air-to-air missile
> *Dimensions:* diameter 0.157m (6.18in); length 2.77m (109.06in); span 0.668m (26.30in)
> *Weight:* total round 89.8kg (198.0lb)
> *Warhead:* 12.5kg (27.6lb) blast fragmentation
> *Powerplant:* one SNPE Roméo single-stage double-base solid propellant rocket
> *Performance:* speed about Mach 3; range 320/10,000m (350/10,935yd)
> *Guidance:* SAT AD3601 infra-red homing

Developed from 1968, initially as a private-venture competitor to the US AIM-9 Sidewinder missile, but then accepted by the French Air Ministry for official development as the primary short range missile armament of French fighters, the **Matra R550 Magic** was designed for unrestricted 140° rear hemisphere engagement of targets at altitudes of up to 18,000m (59,055ft), the engagement envelope being limited above this altitude. Before launch the Magic's lead sulphide seeker is cooled (and thus made more sensitive) by liquid nitrogen in a bottle inside the launch rail, and the missile can be launched by an aircraft manoeuvring at +6g at any speed between 0 and 1,300km/hr (808mph). Particularly useful features of the R550's design are the capabilities for launch at ranges down to 300m (985ft) and to cross safely only 50m (165ft) in front of the launch aircraft. This provides any Magic-carrying fighter with the ability to engage targets of opportunity appearing on the fighter's 'unarmed' side. The warhead is located in the centre of the body, and the triple set of cruciform aerodynamic surfaces includes freely-rotating fins at the rear, fixed delta canards near the nose and, just aft of these canards, powered control surfaces of an angular and highly distinctive shape. The R550 series is generally associated with fighters of French design, but is installationally interchangeable with the Sidewinder.

Entering service in the mid-1980s, the **R550 Magic 2** is an improved version of the baseline model (since redesignated Magic 1) with a real all-aspect engagement capability through the adoption of a multi-element infra-red seeker of much improved sensitivity, a new radar proximity fuse, an improved SNPE Richard motor, and a combination of greater structural strength and better aerodynamic controls for enhanced dogfight manoeuvrability. Moreover, the seeker can be slaved to the radar of Dassault-Breguet Mirage 2000 fighters to provide optimum firing conditions.

Right:
The Dassault-Breguet Lancier prototype shows off part of its weapon capability in the form of two Matra R550 Magic air-to-air missiles and one Aérospatiale AM39 Exocet anti-ship missile, together with an underwing drop tank. *Dassault-Breguet*

Above:

Potent self-defence capability is given to the SEPECAT Jaguar International by a pair of Matra Magic air-to-air missiles carried on unusual overwing hardpoints. This leaves the underwing points free for offensive ordnance such as that seen here in the form of BL755 cluster bombs (inboard) and Matra 155 rocket-launchers (outboard). *BAe AWFA671*

MATRA MICA

> *Type:* short/medium range air-to-air missile
> *Dimensions:* diameter 0.152m (6.0in); length 3.10m (122.05in)
> *Weight:* total round 110kg (242.5lb)
> *Warhead:* ?kg (?lb) Thomson Brandt blast fragmentation
> *Powerplant:* one SNPE solid propellant rocket
> *Performance:* speed Mach 4; range ?/50km (?/31.1 miles)
> *Guidance:* strapdown inertial plus infra-red or semi-active radar
> homing

Due to enter service in the 1990s as France's most important short and medium range air-to-air missile, the **Matra MICA** (Missile d'Interception et de Combat Aérien, or interception and air combat missile) was first fired in trials during 1982. It is similar in appearance to the US RIM-66/RIM-67 Standard series of surface-to-air missiles, but of course much smaller. The type is designed to equip all current and projected French fighters, and combines the capabilities of other Western air-to-air missiles such as the AIM-120A AMRAAM and AIM-132A ASRAAM. The MICA is designed for great agility (more than the 50g capability of the Magic, and this allows turns immediately after launch to engage targets on any bearing from the launch aircraft other than dead astern), and uses thrust-vector control until motor burn-out, after which the aerodynamic tail controls are used. The MICA is designed for launch on the basis of the parent aircraft's primary sensor, cruising under strapdown inertial guidance and receiving updates on target position via a datalink before the seeker is activated in the final stages of the engagement. The MICA has a choice of two seekers (the IR type being used for shorter-range air combat and the semi-active radar type being used for longer-ranged interception), while its comparatively small size allows aircraft such as the Dassault-Breguet Mirage 2000 to carry as many as six missiles. The three primary tasks are defined as long range interception using the combination of inertial guidance, datalink update and terminal homing; medium range interception using inertial guidance and terminal homing; and short range (dogfighting) interception with the terminal homing locked on to the target before missile launch.

MATRA MISTRAL

> *Type:* short range air-to-air missile
> *Dimensions:* diameter 0.09mm (3.54in); length 1.80m (70.87in)
> *Weight:* total round 17kg (37.48lb)
> *Warhead:* 3kg (6.61lb) Thomson Brandt blast fragmentation
> *Powerplant:* one SNPE dual-thrust solid propellant rocket
> *Performance:* speed Mach 2.6; range 300/6,000m (330/6,560yd)
> *Guidance:* infra-red homing

Otherwise known as the **AATCP** (Air-Air Très Courte Portée, or air-to-air very short range) missile, the **Matra Mistral** is the air-launched version of the SATCP (Sol-Air Très Courte Portée, or surface-to-air very short range) missile. This is an extremely capable tube-launched weapon designed for carriage mainly by helicopters, which can lift up to four twin-tube launchers with eyelid doors to protect the missile's seeker head up to the moment of launch. The Mistral can be used for offensive as well as defensive purposes, and targets can be acquired with the helicopter's basic missile sight or, in advanced types, by a crew member's helmet-mounted sight. In both cases the target can be indicated to the missile before launch, as can also the seeker's scanning pattern. After launching the missile the helicopter can turn away as the Mistral covers its maximum 3,000m (3,280yd) range in a mere 5sec against a target manoeuvring at up to 8g.

ISRAEL

RAFAEL PYTHON 3

Type: short range dogfighting air-to-air missile
Dimensions: diameter 0.16m (6.3in); length 3.00m (118.11in); span 0.86m (33.86in)
Weight: total round 120kg (264.6lb)
Warhead: 11kg (24.25lb) blast fragmentation
Powerplant: one Rafael Armaments Authority double-base solid propellant rocket
Performance: speed Mach 3; range 500/15,000m (545/16,405yd)
Guidance: infra-red homing

Developed from the late 1970s as the Shafrir 3, the **Rafael Python 3** is a development of the Shafrir with an improved motor for greater range, a seeker with improved sensitivity for all-aspect engagement capability, and aerodynamic improvements for better agility. The close relationship of the Python and of its predecessor to the Sidewinder is shown by the Israeli missiles' use of Sidewinder-type slipstream-driven 'rollerons' on the rectangular tail surfaces to prevent roll and so ease the task of the guidance system, which works through a cruciform of delta canards indexed in line with the tail surfaces. The Python 3 is claimed to offer engagement capabilities comparable to those of the AIM-9L variant of the Sidewinder.

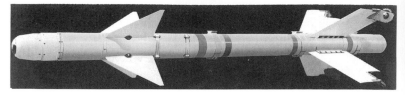

Above:

Despite a number of significant differences, the Rafael Python 3 is clearly related to the Shafrir 2, itself markedly similar to the American AIM-9 Sidewinder in features such as general layout and 'rollerons'.
Rafael Armament Development

ISRAEL

RAFAEL SHAFRIR 2

Type: short range dogfighting air-to-air missile
Dimensions: diameter 0.16m (6.3in); length 2.47m (97.24in); span 0.52m (20.47in)
Weight: total round 93kg (205.0lb)
Warhead: 11kg (24.25lb) blast fragmentation
Powerplant: one Rafael Armaments Authority double-base solid propellant rocket
Performance: speed Mach 2.5; range 500/5,000m (545/5,470yd)
Guidance: infra-red homing

Derived from a preproduction Shafrir 1, the **Rafael Shafrir 2** entered Israeli service in 1969 and is a capable short range missile that has performed well in combat with a claimed 65/70 'kill' percentage. The weapon is based in concept on the AIM-9 Sidewinder, but from the start of development in 1961 it was decided to increase the diameter of the body in comparison with that of the American weapon and thereby simplify the engineering of the weapon, as well as making possible the use of a larger warhead containing 4kg (8.8lb) of explosive. The missile has the same basic layout as the Python 3, with control effected by the cruciform of canard surfaces which are pneumatically actuated to operate in pairs.

SELENIA ASPIDE

Type: medium/long range air-to-air missile
Dimensions: diameter 0.203m (8.0in); length 3.70m (145.67in); span
  1.00m (39.37in)
Weight: total round 220kg (485.0lb)
Warhead: 33kg (72.75lb) Difesa e Spazio blast fragmentation
Powerplant: one SNIA-Viscosa single-stage solid propellant rocket
Performance: speed Mach 4; range 100km (62.1 miles) from a
  high-altitude launch decreasing to 50km (31.07 miles) from a
  low-altitude launch
Guidance: Selenia monopulse semi-active radar homing

Developed from 1969 on the conceptual basis of the Raytheon AIM-7E
Sparrow, the **Selenia Aspide** is like the American missile in being a
multi-role type (with important ground-to-air and ship-to-air applications in
the Spada and Albatros air-defence systems respectively), and entered
air-to-air service with the Italian Air Force in 1979. The type arms the Aeritalia
F-104S and Panavia Tornado and, matched to I-band monopulse radar, has
greater low-altitude range and snap-down capability than the Sparrow,
together with much improved accuracy and resistance to electronic
countermeasures.

BRITISH AEROSPACE SKY FLASH

Type: medium range air-to-air missile
Dimensions: diameter 8.0in (0.203m); length 145.0in (3.683m); span
  40.0in (1.016m)
Weight: total round 425lb (192.8kg)
Warhead: 66lb (29.9kg) blast fragmentation
Powerplant: one Aerojet or Rockwell Mk 52 Mod 2 solid propellant
  rocket
Performance: speed Mach 4; range 31 miles (49.9km) from a
  high-altitude launch
Guidance: Marconi XJ521 monopulse semi-active radar homing

The **British Aerospace Sky Flash** is an advanced British development of
the comparatively short-ranged AIM-7E2 Sparrow with a considerably more
capable monopulse homing system and improved fusing to allow
snap-up/snap-down engagements at all altitudes. Development of the
missile began in 1969, and the resultant weapon retains the classic
aerodynamics of the Sparrow, with a cruciform of delta control wings
mounted on the mid-point of the cylindrical body, and a comparable
cruciform of delta stabilising surfaces at the tail. The weapon entered service
in 1978, and is an extremely accurate missile with warm-up time reduced

Below:
The Saab Viggen can carry a maximum of four RB 71 Sky Flash semi-active radar homing missiles in the air-to-air role, but a more versatile fit is seen here in the form of two RB 71s (inboard) and two RB 24 (AIM-9B Sidewinder) short range missiles (outboard). Sweden also uses the AIM-9L version of the Sidewinder with the designation RB 74. *BAe C2132A*

from the American original's 15sec to a tactically advantageous 2sec. The Sky Flash has excellent capabilities against manoeuvring targets, even in conditions of glint and heavy electronic countermeasures, and the type is also used by Sweden with the designation **RB 71**. A consortium of Saab Missiles, Saab Scania Combitech, Ericsson Radio Systems and Volvo Flygmotor is currently modifying existing Swedish stocks to the **RB 71A** standard with an improved motor and guidance system.

Under the company designation **Sky Flash 90**, British Aerospace is working on a development based on the Sky Flash Mk 2 cancelled by the British government in 1981, even though its development was nearly complete, in favour of the AIM-120A AMRAAM. The proposed Sky Flash 90 is designed as a lower-cost answer to the requirements of those countries needing a missile with 'beyond-visual-horizon' capability, and the design is based on a control package using a strapdown inertial platform for mid-course guidance and a Marconi active radar for terminal guidance, plus a Royal Ordnance Hoopoe solid propellant rocket for greater speed and range. These latter factors are aided by thinner wings and a new low-drag rear end to the missile. Sweden has proposed a Mach 4 or 5 development of this active-homing type with a Volvo Flygmotor ramjet as the **RB 73**. Whether using rocket or ramjet propulsion, the Sky Flash 90/RB 73 is likely to prove an important and popular weapon as its active radar guidance removes the need for the continuous-wave illumination of the target by an expensive radar carried by the basic Sky Flash's launch aircraft. This has to fly on towards the target until the missile has impacted, a course taking the vulnerable aircraft potentially ever farther into airspace protected by surface-to-air as well as air-to-air weapon systems.

USA

RAYTHEON/GENERAL DYNAMICS AIM-7M SPARROW

> *Type:* medium range air-to-air missile
> *Dimensions:* diameter 8.0in (0.203m); length 145.0in (3.683m); span 40.0in (1.016m)
> *Weight:* total round 503lb (228.2kg)
> *Warhead:* 86lb (39kg) Mk 71 blast fragmentation
> *Powerplant:* one Hercules Mk 58 or Aerojet Mk 65 dual-thrust solid propellant rocket
> *Performance:* speed Mach 4; range 62 miles (100km) from a high-altitude launch reducing to 27 miles (43.5km) from a low-altitude launch
> *Guidance:* Raytheon Advanced Monopulse Seeker semi-active radar homing

Introduced in 1962 as the first version of the Sparrow III to enter very large-scale production (the earlier radar beam-riding AIM-7A Sparrow I having totalled 2,000 rounds, the semi-active AIM-7C Sparrow III 2,000 rounds and the liquid propelled AIM-7D Sparrow III 7,500 rounds), the **Raytheon AIM-7E Sparrow III** remains in limited service with several important fighter types. The type is powered by a Rocketdyne Mk 38 Mod 2 or Aerojet Mk 52 single-stage motor for a burn-out speed of Mach 3.7, weighs 452lb (205kg), and has a range of 28 miles (44km) with its 66lb (30kg) warhead, whose casing breaks into some 2,600 fragments on detonation, spreading outward at more than 1,700ft (518m)/sec to provide a lethal radius of 400ft (122m). The missile is guided by Raytheon continuous-wave semi-active radar guidance matched to a number of radars. This variant of the Sparrow III was also built in Italy by Selenia, and a limited-production shorter-range and more manoeuvrable version was produced in the USA as the **AIM-7E2 Sparrow**. The latter was developed in response to a requirement of the Vietnam War, in which US fighters were seldom able to use the comparatively long-ranged AIM-7E Sparrow because of the political constraint on firing missiles against aircraft which had not been visually identified. The AIM-7E2 thus has a reduced minimum range, and the opportunity was taken to provide aerodynamic surfaces that could be plugged in rather than requiring attachment with the aid of special tools. The definitive version still in service is the **AIM-7E3 Sparrow**, which is a conversion of the AIM-7E2 with improved reliability and greater target-sensing capability.

The **AIM-7F Sparrow** is a much redesigned version introduced in 1977 on the McDonnell Douglas F-15 Eagle and now carried also by the McDonnell Douglas F/A-18 Hornet. Whereas the AIM-7E has its forward body as far aft as the wings filled with guidance equipment (homing head and autopilot), trailed aft of the wings by a comparatively small warhead and a short motor, the AIM-7F uses the advantages of more compact solid-state electronics to reduce guidance package volume by some 40%, allowing a larger warhead to be incorporated in the space thus made empty in front of the wings, and a longer motor to be used in the whole portion aft of the wings. The variant thus has a much larger engagement envelope through the adoption of solid-state electronics and a Mk 58 or Mk 65 dual-thrust motor. Like the AIM-7E it is 144.0in (3.658m) long, but weighs 503lb (228kg) and has a 86lb (39kg) warhead. The use of continuous-wave and pulse-Doppler guidance with a conical-scan slotted antenna considerably enhances look-down/shoot-down capability, even at the longer ranges possible with the variant. The AIM-7F also possesses superior resistance to electronic countermeasures.

Introduced in 1982 as an interim variant pending availability of the AIM-120 AMRAAM, the **AIM-7M Sparrow** has a new digital monopulse seeker offering performance comparable with that of the British Sky Flash derivative, especially in the longer-range look-down/shoot-down mode. The variant also offers other electronic and engineering improvements to bring down production cost while enhancing reliability and performance at low altitude and in ECM environments. The type also possesses a warhead of greater lethality than those of earlier Sparrows.

Under development in the late 1980s by Raytheon, the **AIM-7P Sparrow** is the latest development of the basic Sparrow III air-to-air missile. No details of the programme have been released, but it is likely that the development is centred on electronic rather than aerodynamic or powerplant features.

Right:
In the stand-off interception role, these McDonnell Douglas Phantoms of the RAF carry four AIM-7 Sparrow medium range air-to-air missiles semi-recessed under the lower fuselage, and four AIM-9 Sidewinder short range air-to-air missiles in pairs under the wings. *John Dunnell*

Above:
A McDonnell Douglas Phantom FGR Mk 2 of No 56 Squadron from RAF Wattisham reveals the load for a training sortie: training versions of the AIM-7 Sparrow and AIM-9 Sidewinder air-to-air missiles, and an SUU-23/A 20mm cannon pod on the centreline.
John Dunnell

FORD AEROSPACE/RAYTHEON AIM-9L SIDEWINDER

Type: short range dogfighting air-to-air missile
Dimensions: diameter 5.0in (0.127m); length 112.2in (2.85m); span 24.8in (0.63m)
Weight: total round 188lb (85.3kg)
Warhead: 22.5lb (10.2kg) blast fragmentation
Powerplant: one Thiokol or Bermite Mk 36 Model 7/8, or reduced-smoke TX-683 solid propellant rocket
Performance: speed Mach 2.5; range 19,360yd (17,700m)
Guidance: Bodensee Gerätetechnik/Ford ALASCA infra-red homing

Still in the operational inventory of a few nations (some 80,000 missiles of this variant having been built), the **Ford AIM-9B Sidewinder** is 111.4in (2.83m) long, spans 21.0in (0.559m) and entered service in 1956 with a 10lb (4.54kg) blast fragmentation warhead plus infra-red proximity fuse. From 1982 the fuse has been replaced with the Hughes DSU-21/B active laser fuse in all missiles carrying this warhead, namely the AIM-9B, E, J, N and P variants. The missile has a target-acquisition angle of 25° and a 4° seeker field of vision. Powered by a Naval Propellant Plant-designed — but Aerojet-built — Mk 17 motor, the 155lb (70.3kg) missile achieves a range of 3,500yd (3,200m). The **AIM-9B/FWG.2** is an improved European-built model with greater seeker sensitivity. Its length is 114.5in (2.908m), but though weight increases to 167lb (75.8kg) the range is boosted to 4,000yd (3,660m); the missile is used by Sweden with the designation **RB 24**. The **AIM-9E** is a US-built improvement with a Ford thermo-electrically cooled seeker (again for greater sensitivity) plus 'revitalisation' of the existing electronics, and the length of the missile is 118.1in (3.00m), with weight 164lb (74.4kg) and range 4,575yd (4,185m) within a considerably expanded operational envelope. The AIM-9E began to enter service in 1967, and a version with a reduced-smoke motor is designated **AIM-9E2**. Some of the original weapons have been converted with reduced-smoke motors with the designation **AIM-9B2**, and are used for special mission or training.

Introduced in 1967, **AIM-9G Sidewinder** is an improved version of the US Navy's 1965 **AIM-9D Sidewinder** (the real precursor of the latest Sidewinder variants and fitted with the Raytheon Mk 18 Mod 1 infra-red seeker) with an infra-red/radar-proximity fused 22.4lb (10.2kg) continuous-rod HE warhead, the Thiokol Mk 36 solid propellant motor and the so-called Sidewinder Expanded Acquisition Mode (SEAM) seeker for improved target acquisition and engagement capability, especially at low altitude. This variant is 113.0in (2.87m) long and has a fin span of 24.8in (0.63m), and at a weight of 191lb (86.6kg) has a range of 19,360yd (17,705m).

Introduced in 1970, the **AIM-9H Sidewinder** is a 186lb (84.4kg) missile developed on the basis of the AIM-9G with the same warhead, the Mk 36 Mod 6 motor, an improved solid-state and cryogenically-cooled seeker providing enhanced tracking speed and all-weather capability, and other modifications to improve manoeuvrability. The type is dimensionally

Above:
Four plus four is the norm for many US fighters; this McDonnell Douglas F-15A Eagle is sporting four AIM-7M Sparrows carried tangentially on the lower corners of the inlet trunks, and a pair of AIM-9L/M Sidewinders under each wing. *McDonnell Douglas C22-395-33*

Below:
Typical of the installation on lighter combat aircraft, these AIM-9L/M Sidewinders are carried on the wingtip launchers of a General Dynamics F-16A Fighting Falcon, leaving the underwing hardpoints free for other ordnance or for another four Sidewinders if a dedicated air-combat mission is planned.
General Dynamics 31-36336

identical with the AIM-9G and possesses the same range, but introduced more powerful actuators to provide greater manoeuvrability.

The **AIM-9J Sidewinder** was developed from the AIM-9E by converting obsolescent AIM-9Bs (**AIM-9J2**) and making new missiles (**AIM-9J1** and the product-improved **AIM-9J3**). This variant appeared in the mid-1970s and features a Mk 17 solid-propellant motor, a thermo-electrically cooled seeker, some solid-state electronics and revised double-delta control surfaces with more powerful actuators to generate greater manoeuvrability. This model weighs 172lb (78kg), has a length of 120.9in (3.071m) and a span of 22.0in (0.559m), and can reach a range of 15,850yd (14,495m), the reduced range of this version being deemed acceptable because of its considerably higher acceleration.

The **AIM-9L Sidewinder** is a much improved version introduced in 1976, and combines the latest Sidewinder airframe (featuring an upgraded motor and pointed double-delta foreplanes of yet further refined shape for increased manoeuvrability) with a WDU-17/B annular blast/fragmentation warhead and the AM/FM conical-scan seeker developed by Bodensee Gerätetechnik for the abortive Viper AAM (designated TUM-72/B in the USA and offering an excellent all-aspect seeker capability) combined with a dogfighting airframe. The Hughes active optical proximity fusing system incorporates a ring of eight gallium arsenide laser diodes to provide optimum warhead detonation in high-speed manoeuvring combat. The type is used by Sweden with the designation **RB 74**, and is also made under licence in Japan by a consortium headed by Mitsubishi.

The **AIM-9M Sidewinder** is the exclusively US-made version of the AIM-9L with a weight of 189.6lb (86kg) as a result of using a closed-cycle cooler for improved seeker sensitivity (especially at low altitudes), greater resistance to infra-red countermeasures and a 'smokeless' Bermite/Hercules Mk 36 Mod 9 motor for all the tactical advantages of reduced visual signature.

The **AIM-9N Sidewinder** is a redesignation of AIM-9J1 missiles produced by converting AIM-9B and AIM-9E Sidewinders.

The **AIM-9P Sidewinder** is a US-made model (either new-build or upgraded AIM-9B, E and J weapons) to AIM-9L standard with the canards of

Below:
US Air Force groundcrew prepare a batch of AIM-9L Sidewinders for loading on to McDonnell Douglas F-15 Eagle air-superiority fighters. Most of the missiles lack their tail surfaces and characteristic 'rollerons'. *MARS*

the AIM-9J series. The variant also offers greater reliability and a weight of 170lb (77.1kg). There are four subvariants in the form of the **AIM-9P1** with an acive optical proximity fuse, the **AIM-9P2** with the 'smokeless' motor, the **AIM-9P3** combining AIM-9P1 and AIM-9P2 features with a new warhead of reduced thermal sensitivity and greater shelf life, and the **AIM-9P4** 'security assistance missile' for the US Air Force with increased target-acquisition and tracking capabilities combined with an advanced fuse.

The **AIM-9R Sidewinder** is a 193lb (87.5kg) derivative of the AIM-9M (and originally designated **Improved AIM-9M**) under development for production from 1988 with a radically upgraded seeker (of the imaging infra-red variety that does away with the seeker cooling of all other recent Sidewinder variants) for greater acquisition range and better resistance to countermeasures. The type also has an active laser proximity fuse and a range of 21,125yd (19,315m).

Below:
A McDonnell Douglas AV-8B Harrier II is shown off with just part of its 9,200lb (4,173kg) ordnance load. From front to rear the weapons are four Sidewinders (on the left a training store and an AIM-9L, and on the right a pair of AIM-9Gs), four 577lb (262kg) LAU-10 and six 216lb (98kg) LAU-68 launchers for 2.75in (70mm) rockets, six LAU-10 and four LAU-68 launchers, 10 Mk 77 520lb (236kg) bombs, 10 Mk 20 'Rockeye' 490lb (222kg) cluster bombs, 15 Mk 81 250lb (113kg) free-fall bombs, 16 Mk 82 500lb (227kg) bombs and a triple ejector rack for another trio of Mk 82s, six Mk 83 1,000lb (454kg) bombs, and four triple ejector racks. The Harrier II can also lift a substantial number of air-to-surface guided weapons. *McDonnell Douglas C12-11175-7*

USA

HUGHES AIM-54A PHOENIX

> *Type:* long range air-to-air missile
> *Dimensions:* diameter 15.0in (0.381m); length 157.8in (4.008m); span 36.4in (0.925m)
> *Weight:* total round 985lb (446.8kg)
> *Warhead:* 132lb (59.9kg) continuous-rod blast fragmentation
> *Powerplant:* one Aerojet Mk 60 or Rocketdyne Mk 47 Mk 0 single-stage solid-propellant rocket
> *Performance:* speed Mach 4.3+; range 2.4/125+ miles (3.86/201.2+km)
> *Guidance:* Hughes DSQ-26 package with strapdown inertial for the early phase, semi-active radar homing for the cruise phase and active radar for the terminal phase

Designed for the abortive General Dynamics F-111B swing-wing naval fighter, the **Hughes AIM-54A Phoenix** was brought into service together with the associated Hughes AWG-9 pulse-Doppler fire-control system in the Grumman F-14 Tomcat fleet-defence fighter. The type retains the classic aerodynamics of Hughes's earlier air-to-air missiles, with a substantial body carrying a cruciform of low-aspect-ratio delta wings located well aft and trailed by rectangular control surfaces indexed in line with the wings. The large body diameter allows the use of a wide-diameter radar antenna in the nose radome, and also provides volume for the missile's other primary components. From front to rear these are the electronics (radar avionics, guidance package and proximity fuse system), the warhead, the rocket motor, and (round the nozzle) the autopilot and control-surface hydraulic actuators. After launch the missile climbs to a maximum altitude of some 81,400ft (24,810m), cruising under control of the onboard autopilot with guidance of the semi-active type using reflections of the radar in launch aircraft's AWG-9 system. This high-altitude cruise maximises range by reducing drag and providing the rocket with optimum operating conditions, and as the missile dives down to the attack the energy potential of the cruise altitude is converted into kinetic energy for greater manoeuvrability in the terminal phase of the flight. The missile's radar switches to the active mode for the final 20,000yd (18,290m) of the attack, the availability of three fusing modes offering maximum target-destruction capability. The Phoenix began to enter service in 1973. Notable features of the missile and fire-control combination are exceptional range, and the ability to engage six targets simultaneously (using a time-share system so that the AWG-9 can control the missiles, which can lose touch with the radar for 14sec before failing to reacquire the designated target) regardless of weather conditions and target aspect. Production continued up to 1980, by which time some 2,566 rounds had been made.

The **AIM-54B Phoenix** version entered production in late 1977, and is in essence a product-improved AIM-54A with aerodynamic surfaces of sheet metal rather than honeycomb construction, non-liquid hydraulic and thermal-conditioning systems, and simplified engineering to ease production.

Developed from 1977 and introduced in 1982, the **AIM-54C Phoenix** is a considerably improved missile with digital rather than analog electronics, a new Nortronics strapdown inertial reference unit, solid-state radar and very much more capable electronic counter-countermeasures capability. The weight of this variant is 1,008lb (457kg), the speed Mach 5 and the ceiling 100,000+ft (30,490m). As with the AIM-54A, legend range has been considerably exceeded in service, especially when the F-14 launch aircraft is supported by a Grumman E-2C Hawkeye warning and control system aircraft.

Missile homing methods (right)

Tomcat/Phoenix cruise missile interception trial (centre)
Sea-skimming cruise missiles pose particularly severe problems for major surface forces. The missiles can cruise at high subsonic speed very close to the water, and are very difficult to detect even at short range. In this significant test a Tomcat/Phoenix combination detected, engaged and destroyed a BQM-34A drone flying some 10,000ft (3,050m) below it

Below:
Grumman technicians practise the loading of dummy AIM-54A Phoenix missiles on to the F-14A mock-up, in the process revealing the size of these major missiles, and the considerable underfuselage area required for the standard fit of four such missiles. *Grumman 69614*

Tomcat/Phoenix manoeuvring target interception trial (right)
Successful interception by a missile has often been avoided when the target performs violent manoeuvres in the missile's terminal attack phase. In this trial the QF-86 drone was rolled at high *g* into a steep dive just 16sec after the Phoenix had been launched, but failed to shake off the AIM-54A even after it was extricated from the dive in an even higher-*g* pull-out

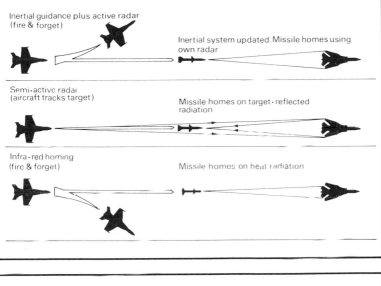

Inertial guidance plus active radar
(fire & forget)

Inertial system updated. Missile homes using own radar

Semi·active radar
(aircraft tracks target)

Missile homes on target·reflected radiation

Infra·red homing
(fire & forget)

Missile homes on heat radiation

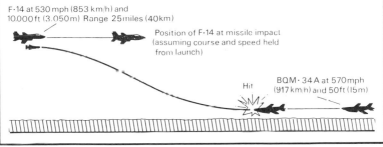

F·14 at 530 mph (853 km/h) and 10.000 ft (3.050m) Range 25 miles (40km)

Position of F·14 at missile impact (assuming course and speed held from launch)

BQM·34A at 570 mph (917 km/h) and 50 ft (l5m)

Hit

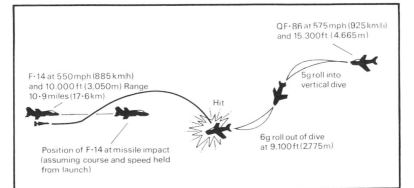

QF·86 at 575 mph (925 km/h) and 15.300 ft (4.665m)

F·14 at 550 mph (885 km/h) and 10.000 ft (3,050m) Range 10·9 miles (17·6km)

5g roll into vertical dive

Hit

Position of F·14 at missile impact (assuming course and speed held from launch)

6g roll out of dive at 9,100 ft (2,775m)

Tomcat/Phoenix 'one-against-six' interception trial

The combination of the Tomcat fighter with Phoenix missiles undertook and passed its most rigorous test with the simultaneous engagement of six targets flying at much the same altitude but at differing speeds (Mach 0.6 to Mach 1.1) and across a 17.25 mile (27.75km) front; of the six Phoenixes launched in 38sec, three scored direct hits, one secured a 'lethal-radius' success, one missed, and the last was a 'no-test' failure, giving an overall success rate of 80%

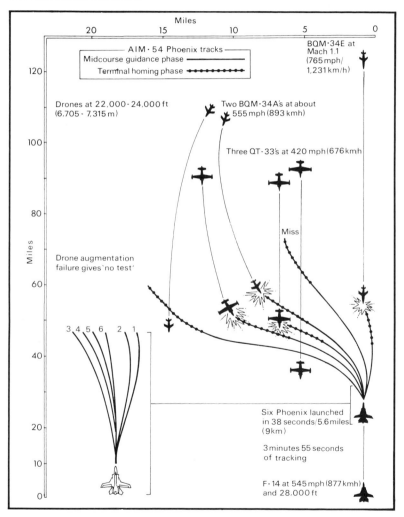

Right:

A decisive moment in its development programme: the first launch of an AIM-120A AMRAAM from a General Dynamics F-16 Fighting Falcon in December 1984. *General Dynamics 31-17768*

USA

HUGHES AIM-120A AMRAAM

Type: medium range air-to-air missile
Dimensions: diameter 7.0in (0.178m); length 143.9in (3.655m); span 24.7in (0.627m)
Weight: total round 335.2lb (152.05kg)
Warhead: 45lb (20.4kg) blast fragmentation
Powerplant: one solid propellant rocket
Performance: speed about Mach 4; range 45 miles (72km) from a high-altitude launch declining to 34 miles (55km) from a low-altitude launch
Guidance: Nortronics strapdown inertial for mid-course phase, and Hughes active radar for terminal phase

Designed in the late 1970s and early 1980s for a service debut in the late 1980s as replacement for the AIM-7F/M variants of the Sparrow, the **Hughes AIM-120A AMRAAM** (Advanced Medium Range Air-to-Air Missile) is a fire-and-forget BVR (Beyond-Visual-Range) weapon with size and weight little more than those of the AIM-9 Sidewinder but capabilities and performance better than those of the considerably larger Sparrow. The missile is launched from a standard rail, and cruises on a preprogrammed course (with mid-course update from the launch aircraft's radar when necessary) until it reaches the vicinity of the target. Here the onboard system activates the missile's active radar seeker, which also possesses a 'home-on-jam' mode. The whole programme has been bedevilled by technical problems, cost overruns and political antipathy, and service entry has been delayed to 1989 or 1990.

3: Air-to-Surface Missiles

FRANCE

AÉROSPATIALE AS11

Type: lightweight air-to-surface missile
Dimensions: diameter 0.164m (6.46in); length 1.201m (47.28in); span 0.50m (19.69in)
Weight: total round 29.9kg (65.92lb)
Warhead: ?kg (?lb) Type 140AC hollow-charge anti-tank, or Type 140AP02 penetrating blast fragmentation, or Type 140AP59 blast fragmentation, or Type 140CCN anti-ship varieties
Powerplant: one SNPE Simplet solid-propellant booster rocket and one SNPE Sophie solid-propellant sustainer rocket
Performance: speed increases from 360 to 684km/hr (224 to 425mph) in the cruise phase of the flight; range 3,500/7,000m (3,830/7,655yd)
Guidance: wire command to line of sight

The **Aérospatiale AS11** is the helicopter-borne version of the SS11 surface-launched anti-tank missile, and can be used for a number of tactical applications depending on the type of warhead fitted. The weapon is obsolete as an anti-tank weapon (taking as long as 21sec to reach its maximum range), but when used with a gyro-stabilised-sight is still effective as a bunker-buster and for attacks on naval targets such as landing craft. The basic weapon was developed between 1953 and 1955 as the Nord 5210, and was first adopted for helicopter use in 1958. Enormously successful in commercial terms, the SS11/AS11 series was produced to the extent of some 180,000 missiles for sale to armed forces in at least 30 countries, many of whom still use the weapon. The Type 140AC warhead can penetrate 140mm (5.51in) of armour, the Type 140AP02 detonates 2.6kg (5.72lb) of HE after passing through 10mm (0.4in) of armour, the Type 140AP59 is an impact-fused fragmentation warhead, and the Type 140CCN can deal with landing craft and attack craft.

The **AS11B1** is an improved version with transistorised guidance and the option of TCA infra-red semi-automatic command to line-of-sight guidance.

AÉROSPATIALE AS12

Type: air-to-surface missile
Dimensions: diameter 0.21m (8.27in); length 1.87m (73.62in); span 0.65m (25.6in)
Weight: total round 76kg (167.5lb)
Warhead: 28.4kg (62.6lb) OP3C penetrating blast fragmentation
Powerplant: one SNPE Achille solid-propellant booster rocket and one SNPE Hermioné solid propellant sustainer rocket
Performance: speed 338km/hr (210mph); range 8,000m (8,750yd)
Guidance: wire command to line of sight

The **Aérospatiale AS12** is the air-launched version of the SS12 which entered service in 1955 as a scaled-up version of the SS11 specifically for use against bunkers and warships, and is now of only limited use even in these two roles. Compared with its predecessor, the AS12's key features are double the range and four times the destructive power. The OP3C warhead can detonate a 28.4kg (63lb) charge after penetrating 40mm (1.57in) of armour.

51

FRANCE

AÉROSPATIALE AS30 LASER

Type: air-to-surface missile
Dimensions: diameter 0.342m (13.46in); length 3.65m (143.7in); span 1.00m (39.37in)
Weight: total round 520kg (1,146.4lb)
Warhead: 240kg (529.1lb) blast fragmentation or semi-armour-piercing HE
Powerplant: one SNPE/Aérospatiale two-stage (composite booster and cast double-base sustainer) solid-propellant rocket
Performance: speed Mach 1.5; range 3,000 to 11,250m (3,280 to 12,305yd)
Guidance: strapdown inertial for mid-course phase, and Thomson-CSF Ariel semi-active laser for terminal phase

Introduced in 1960 as the Nord 5401 to provide French Dassault Mirage IIIE fighter-bombers with a moderate stand-off capability, the **Aérospatiale AS30** is essentially a scaled-up version of the out-of-service AS20. The missile has four delta wings located as a cruciform arrangement mid-way along the body, and its use allows the launch aircraft to come no closer than 3,000m (3,280yd) to the target, the operator then radio-commanding the missile to the visual line of sight with an accuracy of less than 10m (33ft). The weapon is 3.839m (151.14in) long with the X12 warhead, or 3.885m (152.95in) long with the X35 warhead.

Introduced in 1964 exclusively for French tactical aircraft, the **AS30TCA** is a development of the AS30 with semi-automatic command to line-of-sight guidance removing the need for the operator to track both the missile and the target, which is a severe tactical disadvantage for the AS30 model. The guidance system for this variant uses an aircraft-carried SAT device to keep track of the flare at the rear of the missile. Another modification is the installation of four rear-mounted flick-open fins, indexed in line with the wings, to replace the control spoilers in the two exhaust nozzles.

Introduced in 1985 after programme launch in 1978 and a first firing in 1980, the **AS30 Laser** is a much-improved model designed for use with the Thomson-CSF/Martin Marietta ATLIS 2 pod, allowing the aircraft to launch and break away while the laser pod under the fuselage or wing continues to designate the locked-in target for the missile, whose maximum flight time is 21sec. The main carriers of the missile are the Dassault Mirage F1 and Mirage 2000, and the SEPECAT Jaguar A. The warhead has a hardened steel casing and, in combination with an impact speed of 1,620km/hr (1,007mph), this provides the missile with the capability to penetrate 2.0m (6.56ft) of concrete before detonating.

FRANCE

AÉROSPATIALE ASMP

Type: air-launched cruise missile
Dimensions: diameter about 0.42m (16.54in) and width across inlets
    about 0.82m (32.28in); length 5.38m (211.81in); span 0.956m (37.6in)
Weight: total round 900kg (1,984.1lb)
Warhead: ?kg (?lb) 100/150kt nuclear
Powerplant: one integral solid-propellant booster rocket and one
    ramjet sustainer
Performance: speed Mach 4; range 300km (186 miles)
Guidance: Sagem inertial and terrain-following

Designed from 1978 (after an abortive beginning from 1971 as the armament
of the proposed Dassault Mirage G and cancelled Dassault Super Mirage),
the **Aérospatiale ASMP** (Air-Sol Moyenne Portée, or medium range
air-to-surface) weapon is an air-launched cruise missile optimised for
carriage by the Dassault-Breguet Mirage IVP bomber, after conversion from
Mirage IVA standard with an armament of one free-fall nuclear weapon; also
the Dassault-Breguet Mirage 2000N low-altitude strike aircraft and the
Dassault-Breguet Super Etendard carrier-borne strike fighter. The ASMP
is essentially a slim cylindrical weapon with a cruciform of modestly swept
control fins at its rear, but a singular appearance is afforded by the lateral
inlet trunks for the ramjet portion of the propulsion arrangement. The ASMP
entered service in 1986, and provides the French air forces with a stand-off
nuclear capability against large targets such as railway yards, main bridges,
and command communications centres. The type can fly a high-altitude
profile ending with a steep supersonic dive, or alternatively a low-altitude
terrain-following profile of shorter range.

This picture:
Using JATO units to provide adequate take-off characteristics at high weight, this Dassault-Breguet Mirage IVP carries an ASMP operational-level cruise missile. *Dassault-Breguet*

MATRA BGL 400

Type: air-to-surface laser-guided glide bomb
Dimensions: diameter 0.403m (15.87in); length 3.402m (133.94in);
  span 0.789m (31.06in)
Weight: total round 475kg (1,045.2lb)
Warhead: 400kg (882lb) bomb
Powerplant: none
Performance: speed high subsonic; range 10,000m (10,935yd)
Guidance: Thomson-CSF TMV 630 Eblis semi-active laser homing

The **Matra BGL** series is the French equivalent to the US 'Paveway' series,
comprising standard low-drag general-purpose bombs to which are fitted a
nose-mounted laser guidance package plus control fins, and a tail-mounted
assembly of folding wings to increase range. Currently under development,
the **BGL 250** is a standard French 250kg (551lb) bomb with the same type of
laser homing and flight-control system as that used on the in-service BGL 400
series. The diameter of the weapon is 0.228m (8.98in), length 3.329m
(131.07in) and span 0.64m (25.2in).

The **BGL 400** is a useful weapon in service with the French Air Force and
several export customers. It is thus a standard 400kg (882lb) bomb provided
with cruciform wings/fins on a rearward extension of the bomb's body and
fitted with a seeker/control section on the nose. The laser seeker is based on
the Ariel unit of the AS30 Laser missile, and the target can be designed from
the ground or by an aircraft using the ATLIS designator system, allowing a
lock-on range of between 4,000 and 10,000m (4,375 and 10.935yd). The
weapon is designed for release at between 50 and 150m (165 and 490ft) by
aircraft flying at speeds up to 1,100km/hr (684mph).'

The **BGL 1000** is a considerably larger version of the same BGL series, but
in this instance based on the standard 1,000kg (2,205lb) bomb, with a
diameter of 0.457m (18.0in), a length of 4.212m (165.83in) and a span of
0.90m (35.43in). In 1987 the weapon received the name **Arcole**, and was
revealed as a stand-off weapon with a range of 8,000m (8,750yd) and a
specially strengthened nosecap for the destruction of targets as hard as the
concrete piers of bridges.

Below:
**The Matra BLG series of laser-guided bombs is conceptually akin to the US
'Paveway' series, but use as their core one of the SAMP general-purpose
bombs fitted with a Thomson-CSF Eblis seeker. This is a BLG-400 under the
starboard wing of a Dassault-Breguet Mirage F1.** *Matra*

MATRA/MBB APACHE/CWS

Type: air-launched stand-off dispenser missile
Dimensions: dispenser section is 0.63m (24.8in) wide and 0.48m
(18.9in) high; length 4.04m (159.06in); span 2.53m (99.6in)
Weight: total round 1,000kg (2,204.6lb) for Apache/CWS & 1,150kg
(2,535.3lb) for Apache/CWS II, and 1,220kg (2,689.6lb) for Apache/
CWS III
Warhead: 750kg (1,653.4lb) of submunitions in all three versions
Powerplant: none in Apache/CWS I, one solid-propellant rocket in
Apache/CWS II, and one small turbojet or turbofan in Apache/CWS III
Performance: speed up to Mach 0.95 at launch for all three versions;
range at low altitude 12,000m (13,125yd) for Apache/CWS I, 25/30km
(15.53/18.64 miles) for Apache/CWS II, and 40/50km (25.86/31.07
miles) for Apache/CWS III
Guidance: inertial, or (Apache/CWS III) inertial plus an unspecified
terminal guidance system

The **Matra/MBB Apache/CWS** series of weapons is based on a common airframe, and began life as the Matra Apache and MBB Container Weapon System notions for Belouga and Durandal replacements. The two notions have now been amalgamated into this important family with service entry planned for 1992. Designed for launch at high subsonic speed at an altitude between 50 and 70m (165 and 230ft), the **Apache/CWS I** then glides at between 50 and 100m (165 and 330ft) before descending to release its submunitions from below 50m (165ft). The fuselage is of rectangular section and carries opening wings, a small tailplane and two ventral fins. The box-like central fuselage is 2.0m (6.56ft) long and can be laid out for a number of modular payloads ejected laterally from transverse tubes to cover an area 1,000m (1,095yd) long and 350m (385yd). The submunitions carried in the 42 small or 18 large diameter tubes (or in a variable mix of the two types) are at first to be the same as those used in the MW-1 underfuselage dispenser weapon. The dispenser system bears a close resemblance to the Modular Dispenser System being developed by MBB, and the original CWS was planned to carry any of four payloads (unpowered freight container, unpowered napalm or fuel transporter, unpowered weapon container and powered weapon container), and such a capability could in due course be restored to the Apache/CWS.

The **Apache/CWS II** is the proposed longer range version with a solid propellant rocket to provide greater stand-off range for the launch aircraft when faced with the air-defence capabilities of a sophisticated battlefield. The **Apache/CWS III** is the proposed longest range version with a turbine engine and a terminal guidance system to ensure that the weapon is accurate in the final stages of its long range flight.

Right:
**The modular construction of the Apache/CWS under the structural beam
supporting the flying surfaces and nose-mounted guidance package, allows
the weapon to be configured for an assortment of submunitions.** *Matra*

MATRA MBB COOPERATION

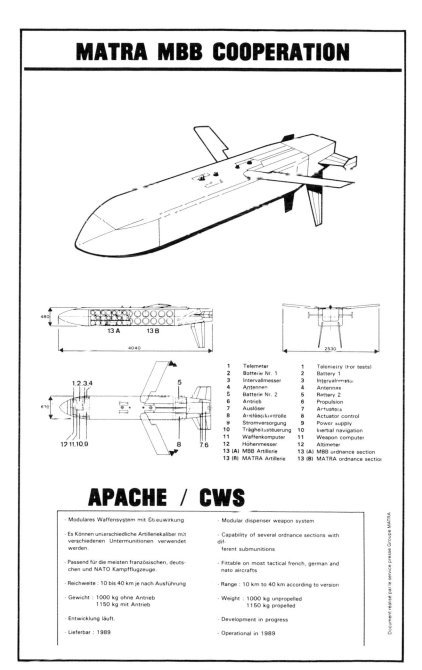

1	Telemeter	1	Telemetry (For tests)
2	Batterie Nr. 1	2	Battery 1
3	Intervallmesser	3	Intervalomstar
4	Antennen	4	Antennas
5	Batterie Nr. 2	5	Battery 2
6	Antrieb	6	Propulsion
7	Auslöser	7	Actuatora
8	Anrlösgskuntrölle	8	Actuator control
9	Stromversorgung	9	Power supply
10	Trägheitusteuerung	10	Inertial navigation
11	Waffenkomputer	11	Weapon computer
12	Höhenmesser	12	Altimeter
13 (A)	MBB Artillerie	13 (A)	MBB ordnance section
13 (B)	MATRA Artillerie	13 (B)	MATRA ordnance sectioi

APACHE / CWS

- Modulares Waffensystem mit Streuwirkung	- Modular dispenser weapon system
- Es Können unterschiedliche Artilleriekaliber mit verschiedenen Untermunitionen verwendet werden.	- Capability of several ordnance sections with different submunitions
- Passend für die meisten französischen, deutschen und NATO Kampfflugzeuge.	- Fittable on most tactical french, german and nato aircrafts
- Reichweite : 10 bis 40 km je nach Ausführung	- Range : 10 km to 40 km according to version
- Gewicht : 1000 kg ohne Antrieb 1150 kg mit Antrieb	- Weight : 1000 kg unpropelled 1150 kg propelled
- Entwicklung läuft.	- Development in progress
- Lieferbar : 1989	- Operational in 1989

DORNIER/AÉROSPATIALE SR-SOM

Type: air-launched short range dispenser missile
Dimensions: length 3.40m (133.86in) for SR-SOM 1 and 4.30m
  (169.3in) for SR-SOM 2; span 2,600mm (102.36in)
Weight: total round 720kg (1,587.3lb) for SR-SOM 1 and 1,400kg
  (3,086.4lb) for SR-SOM 2
Warhead: 350 and 900kg (771.6lb and 1,984.1lb) of submunitions for
  SR-SOM 1 and SR-SOM 2 respectively
Powerplant: one solid propellant rocket
Performance: speed Mach 0.8 at low altitude; range 20km (12.43
  miles) for SR-SOM 1 and 40+km (24.86+ miles) for SR-SOM 2 at low
  altitude
Guidance: as-yet undetermined 'intelligent sensor' mid-course
  guidance and high-precision terminal guidance

Under the programme leadership of the West German company, the
Franco-West German **Dornier/Aérospatiale SR-SOM** (Short Range
Stand-Off Missile) is being developed as an all-weather fire-and-forget
weapon in two forms. The **SR-SOM 1** is planned for lighter tactical aircraft,
and the core of the present design is the **MoBiDiC** (Modular Bird with
Dispenser Container), a modular stand-off weapon schemed on the basis of
Dornier's SR-SOM and Aérospatiale's Pégase II. The payload section and
submunitions have been allocated to Diehl in West Germany and to
Thomson Brandt in France, the proposed submunition type being designed
to give the weapon capability against hardened aircraft shelters and moving
armour. Thomson Brandt had previously studied submunitions for the
Pégase II, these including fuel/air explosive, sensor-aided anti-armour,
anti-runway, anti-vehicle, anti-tank, anti-light armour, and area-denial types
and these may be the basis of the submunitions under development. The
MoBiDiC vehicle is based on a beam supporting the aircraft interface lugs,
rectangular opening wings and tail section (the last incorporating the rocket
motor and opening cruciform tail surfaces). Under this beam is the modular
dispenser with provision for sideways launching of submunitions, and at the
nose is an aerodynamic fairing.

  The **SR-SOM 2** is the larger version of the basic SR-SOM, designed for
higher-performance aircraft and possessing greater range. Also under
evaluation is the possibility of a turbine-engined version for considerably
better range capability.

ISRAELI GUIDED BOMBS

The **Elbit Opher** uses an infra-red homing/control package comparable to that of the US 'Paveway' laser-homing series in performance terms, but considerably cheaper to produce. The package can be added to many types of free-fall ordnance to create 'semi-smart' weapons. A bomb fitted with the Opher package is launched either in a dive attack or using the standard continuously-computed impact point system, and homes on the infra-red radiation from fixed or moving targets. The most common application of the Opher kit is on the Mk 82 500lb (227kg) bomb to produce a weapon 3.43m (135in) long and 325kg (716.5lb) in weight.

More precisely comparable to the 'Paveway' series is the **Israel Aircraft Industries Guillotine**, which is a laser-homing weapon, again based on the locally-produced equivalent to the US Mk 82 bomb. The weapon has a cruciform of spring-out delta tail surfaces, and at the nose the normal type of cylindrical section accommodating the seeker (with automatic search and lock on to reflected laser energy) and the powerful delta control surfaces.

The **Rafael Pyramid** is a more advanced weapon, again based on the warhead of the Mk 82 bomb. The Pyramid has a large rear-mounted cruciform of delta wings, each trailed at its inboard end by a small control surface, and is a low-cost TV-guided bomb weighing about 400kg (882lb).

RAFAEL ARMAMENT DEVELOPMENT AUTHORITY POP-EYE

Type: air-to-surface missile
Dimensions: not revealed
Weight: not revealed
Warhead: not revealed
Powerplant: one solid propellant rocket
Performance: not revealed
Guidance: TV

The **Rafael Pop-Eye** was developed in Israel to meet indigenous as well as export requirements, and was in late 1987 adopted for the US Air Force. No details of this potentially important weapon have yet been revealed.

CASMU (AERITALIA/SNIA BPD) SKYSHARK

> *Type:* air-launched short range dispenser missile
> *Dimensions:* body cross-section 0.394²m (4.24sq ft); length 4.757m
> (187.28in); span 1.50m (59.06in)
> *Weight:* total round 1,050kg (2,314.8lb) for unpowered version and
> 1,170kg (2,579.4lb) for powered versions
> *Warhead:* 745kg (1,642.4lb) of submunitions
> *Powerplant:* (powered versions only) one solid propellant rocket or
> (later) one turbofan
> *Performance:* speed about 975km/h (606mph); range 6,000/12,000m
> (6,560/13,125yd) for unpowered version, or 20/25km (12.43/15.53
> miles) for rocket-powered version, or considerably more than the
> rocket-powered version for the turbofan-powered version
> *Guidance:* unrevealed guidance and fire-control system

The **CASMU Skyshark** is an interesting vehicle developed by a company
formed by Aeritalia and SNIA BPD especially to develop it, CASMU
(Consorzio Armamenti Spendibili Multi Uso, or consortium for multi-role
expendable weapons). The weapon has been designed for stand-off attacks
against high-value targets, and is intended for use by most tactical aircraft. In
its first version the vehicle is a glider carrying a module for laterally-ejected
submunition types, as yet unspecified, but variable for the engagement of
specific targets. CASMU also envisages a rocket-powered medium range
version and ultimately a turbofan-powered long range cruise version. The
tactical keys to the capability of the Skyshark are low radar cross-section
(resulting from the shape of the vehicle and use of radar-absorbent materials
in its structure) and a capable onboard guidance/fire-control system. These
should ensure that the dispenser reaches its target area so that it can then
undertake the high-speed delivery of its submunitions.

SWEDEN

SAAB RB 05A

> *Type:* air-to-surface missile
> *Dimensions:* diameter 0.30m (11.8in); length 3.60m (141.73in); span
> 0.80m (31.50in)
> *Weight:* total round 305kg (672.4lb)
> *Warhead:* ?kg (?lb) Forenarde Fabriksverken blast fragmentation
> *Powerplant:* one prepackaged Volvo Flygmotor VR-35 dual-thrust
> liquid propellant rocket
> *Performance:* speed Mach 1+; range 9,000m (9,845yd)
> *Guidance:* radio command

Introduced in the early 1970s, the **Saab RB 05A** is a substantial and capable air-to-surface missile with supersonic performance. The weapon is designed for use against land and sea targets, and in layout is centred on a slim body with low-aspect-ratio delta wings and, just aft of these, slightly swept control surfaces indexed in line with the wings. The missile is launched at an altitude between 20 and 50m (65 and 165ft) and then, after rapidly accelerating under automatic control to a position straight ahead of the launch aircraft, climbs to an altitude of 400m (1,315ft) as the operator uses a jam-resistant microwave link to guide it to the target, where the blast fragmentation warhead is detonated by a proximity fuse. The missile can be carried by all Swedish attack aircraft, including the small Saab 105.

Below:
The Saab RB 05A is comparatively unusual amongst modern air-to-surface missiles in being supersonic; the missile automatically moves into the pilot's line of sight after launch, and is then guided by microwave link until target impact. This Saab AJ37 Viggen attack aeroplane also carries a pair of launchers for the exceptionally devastating M70 rocket. *Saabfoto 37-0-689*

BRITISH AEROSPACE/MARCONI ALARM

> *Type:* air-to-surface anti-radiation missile
> *Dimensions:* diameter 8.66in (0.22m); length 167.0in (4.242m); span 28.33in (0.72m)
> *Weight:* total round 385lb (174.6kg)
> *Warhead:* ?lb (?kg) MBB blast fragmentation
> *Powerplant:* one Bayern Chemie two-stage solid propellant rocket
> *Performance:* not revealed
> *Guidance:* Marconi passive radar seeking

Based aerodynamically on the Sky Flash air-to-air missile, the **British Aerospace/Marconi ALARM** (Air-Launched Anti-Radiation Missile) should enter service in the late 1980s as the main weapon of British aircraft operating against land- and ship-based radars. The weapon has an advanced and electronically flexible Marconi seeker with four broadband spiral helix receiver antennae (one located in each side of the nose unit), and a computer system that can be pre-programmed with a target priority list, the operating modes and the characteristics of anticipated enemy radars. The seeker's memory allows the ALARM to home even on those radars which have shut down in an effort to break the missile's lock. Several operating modes are possible, though just two have been revealed. In the first the weapon is fired and immediately locks on to a target radar and homes in on it. In the second the weapon zoom climbs to 40,000ft (12,190m) after a low-level launch in the vicinity of any possible target, thereupon descending slowly in a nose-down attitude under a small parachute (offering a loiter of several minutes) as the seeker searches for emissions: once a target has been selected, the parachute is released and the unpowered ALARM dives on to the target. In each case the terminal phase of the attack is made 'down the throat' of the radar to maximise the chances of securing a kinetic as well as explosive 'kill' of the antenna and other components. The missile requires no input from the launch aircraft other than an electrical connection for battery initiation and motor fire as the weapon is launched. The ALARM is thus a true fire-and-forget missile which can be carried by several types of tactical aircraft, the primary British carrier being the BAe Harrier, Panavia Tornado and SEPECAT Jaguar. The missile was originally to have been powered by a Royal Ordnance Nuthatch rocket, but problems with the development of this single-chamber dual-grain powerplant in August 1987 caused BAe to revise the design for a simpler dual-chamber rocket, whose integration will inevitably cause delays to the programme.

Right:
The BAe ALARM anti-radar missile has been bedevilled in its development by engine problems, but offers excellent capabilities and is destined for widespread use by British tactical aircraft. This is a Panavia Tornado GR Mk 1 with seven ALARMs, two drop tanks and two electronic countermeasures pods (an ARI.23246 Sky Shadow jammer under the port wing and a BOZ-100 chaff/flare launcher under the starboard wing). *BAe C3927S*

BRITISH AEROSPACE/MATRA MARTEL AND ARMAT

Type: (AJ168) air-to-surface missile or (AS37 and ARMAT) air-to-surface anti-radiation missile
Dimensions: diameter 15.75in (0.40m); length 152.4in (3.871m) for the AJ168 and 4.12m (162.2in) for the AS37; span 47.25in (1.20m)
Weight: total round 1,213lb (550.2kg) for the AJ168 and 530kg (1,168.4lb) for the AS37
Warhead: 330lb (150kg) blast fragmentation
Powerplant: one Hotchkiss-Brandt/SNPE Basile composite solid propellant booster rocket and one Hotchkiss-Brandt/SNPE Cassandre composite solid propellant sustainer rocket in the AS37, and one SNPE composite boost and cast double-base sustainer rocket in the AJ168
Performance: speed Mach 2; range 60km (37.3 miles) from a high altitude launch declining to 30km (18.6 miles) from a low altitude launch
Guidance: Marconi TV command for the AJ168 or EMD AD37 passive radiation seeker for the AS37

The **Martel** (Missile Anti-Radar TELevision) grew from independent British (Hawker Siddeley Dynamics) and French (Nord) studies in the period from 1960 to 1963, and was then finalised in France and the UK as one of the first European collaborative programmes for service introduction in the late 1960s. The **British Aerospace AJ168** version of the Martel uses command guidance: a small TV camera in the nose of the missile feeds its picture to a screen in front of the operator, who fixes on the target and locks the image into the missile before launching it. The missile then flies under autopilot and altimeter control, being steered by the operator via the data-link pod carried under the launch aircraft's wing. The system provides great accuracy for the delivery of the large warhead. The primary carrier of the missile is the BAe Buccaneer, which can carry three missiles in addition to the data-link pod.

The French version of the Martel is the **Matra AS37**. This was designed for anti-radar use with a broadband passive seeker. This can be used in the air to search through pre-set frequencies for a suitable target (whose operating frequency is then locked into the seeker as the antenna searches through an angle of 90° to localise the target), or locked before take-off if a specific target is to be engaged. Given the rapid evolution of electronics in the 1970s and 1980s, it is not surprising that France has seen fit to develop a more advanced version of the AS37 as the **ARMAT** (Anti-Radar MATra). This differs from the AS37 that it replaces in having a length of 4.15m (163.39in), a span of 1.2m (47.24in), a weight of 550kg (1,212.5lb) including the 160kg (352.7lb) HE warhead, a range of between 15 and 120km (9.3 and 74.6 miles) depending on launch altitude and flight profile, a higher-impulse rocket motor and, most important of all, a more modern and capable ESD passive radar seeker.

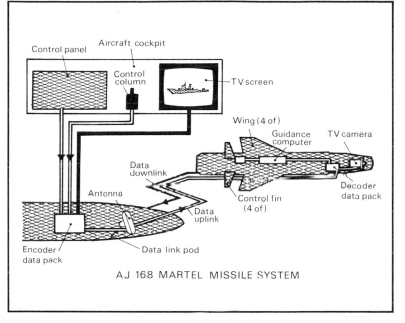

Control panel

Aircraft cockpit

Control column

T V screen

Wing (4 of)

Guidance computer

TV camera

Data downlink

Antenna

Data uplink

Control fin (4 of)

Decoder data pack

Encoder data pack

Data link pod

AJ 168 MARTEL MISSILE SYSTEM

AJ168 Martel missile system

Below:
Seen under the starboard wing of a BAe Buccaneer S Mk 2B are the two versions of the Martel: on the outer hardpoint is the passive radar-homing AS37 and on the inner hardpoint the TV-guided AJ168 with protective cover over its glass nose window. *DAe*

TEXAS INSTRUMENTS AGM-45A SHRIKE

Type: air-to-surface anti-radiation missile
Dimensions: diameter 8.0in (0.203m); length 120.0in (3.048m); span
   36.0in (0.914m)
Weight: total round 390lb (176.9kg)
Warhead: 145lb (65.8kg) blast fragmentation
Powerplant: one Rocketdyne Mk 39 or Aerojet Mk 53 solid propellant
   rocket
Performance: speed Mach 2; range varies with launch altitude and
   speed from 18 to 25 miles (28.95 to 40.25km)
Guidance: Texas Instruments passive radiation seeking

Developed as the ASM-N-10 to meet a US Navy requirement for a simple weapon able to 'take out' enemy land-based radars, the **Texas Instruments AGM-45A Shrike** was introduced in 1963 as the first American tactical anti-radar missile. The weapon was produced in 10 blocks (AGM-45-1 to AGM-45-10), and there are at least 13 different seeker units tailored to individual radar types. This has proved a tactical disadvantage, making it necessary to tune the missile's seeker for a specific radar type before take-off and thus preventing attacks on targets of opportunity, as has the seeker's lack of memory, which cause the missile to 'go ballistic' should the emitter shut down. Detection and localisation of the radar to be engaged is undertaken by the launch aircraft's own electronic countermeasures or electronic support measures systems, the Shrike's seeker being activated only when the operator knows the weapon is within the seeker's frequency capabilities and range.

The **AGM-45B Shrike** is an improved AGM-45A with the Aerojet Mk 78 solid propellant rocket, but retaining the standard configuration of the AGM-45A with a mid-mounted cruciform of high-aspect-ratio control surfaces and a tail-mounted cruciform of low-aspect-ratio fixed fins. The Shrike series is carried by virtually the whole range of US and Israeli tactical aircraft.

Right:
Based aerodynamically and structurally on the AIM-7 Sparrow air-to-air missile, the AGM-45A Shrike is now of only limited value because of its tactically unwieldy guidance system, which uses any one of 13 tailored seeker heads that must be installed before take-off and tuned to a specific frequency. Emitters in other frequencies cannot be engaged, and the missile's lack of memory means that, should a detected emitter close down, the missile will lose lock and 'go ballistic'. *US Navy*

HUGHES AGM-65 MAVERICK

> *Type:* air-to-surface multi-role missile
> *Dimensions:* diameter 12.0in (0.305m); length 98.0in (2.489m); span 28.3in (0.719m)
> *Weight:* total round 463lb (210.0kg) for AGM-65A, 485lb (220.0kg) for AGM-65D, 667lb (302.6kg) for AGM-65E/F and 670lb (303.9kg) for AGM-65G
> *Warhead:* 125lb (56.7kg) Chamberlain shaped charge HE for AGM-65A/B/D, 250lb (113.4kg) Mk 19 blast fragmentation for AGM-65C/F and 300lb (136.1kg) Avco penetrating blast fragmentation for AGM-65E/G
> *Powerplant:* one Thiokol SR109-TC-1 (TX-481) two-stage solid propellant rocket or, from 1981, one Thiokol TX-633 and Aerojet SR115-AJ-1 reduced-smoke solid propellant rocket
> *Performance:* speed supersonic; range 985/26,400yd (900/24,140m)
> *Guidance:* TV imaging for AGM-65A/B, semi-active laser homing for AGM-65C/E and infra-red imaging for AGM-65D/F/G

Development of the **Hughes AGM-65 Maverick** air-to-surface missile began in 1965, and the weapon was introduced in 1972 as a US Air Force air-to-surface missile. The Maverick maintains the standard Hughes configuration, being based on a substantial cylindrical body with a cruciform of swept low-aspect-ratio delta wings, and a cruciform of rectangular control surfaces close-coupled behind the wings. The Maverick series is the smallest fully-guided air-to-surface missile family in the US inventory, and certainly the West's most important weapons of the type, largely because in all its versions it is a fire-and-forget type. The **AGM-65A** is the initial TV imaging version (often known as the **TV Maverick**) and, though a capable weapon, has been found to suffer the tactical disadvantage of low magnification for its nose-mounted camera, forcing the pilot of the launch aircraft to fly close to the target to secure lock-on before missile launch and subsequent automatic attack. The shaped-charge warhead contains 83lb (37.6kg) of explosive, and the accuracy of the AGM-65A (and of the AGM-65D) is about of 5ft (1.5m).

The **AGM-65B Maverick** is an improved TV imaging model introduced in 1980 with double the image magnification of the AGM-65A (based on a 2.5° field of view) to overcome the earlier version's tactical disadvantages. The type is often known as the **Scene-Magnification Maverick**.

The **AGM-65C Maverick** was a highly capable development designed for the battlefield close-support role using Rockwell laser-homing compatible with the ground-based ILS-NT200 as well as the aerial 'Pave Knife', 'Pave Penny', 'Pave Spike', 'Pave Tack' and several non-US designation systems. The weapon was known as the **Laser Maverick**, but was cancelled before reaching full service with the US Marine Corps in the close-support role against targets generally designated by ground-based laser.

The **AGM-65D Maverick** is an imaging infra-red version introduced to US Air Force service in October 1983, and has double the lock-on range of the AGM-65A/B types. The type is capable of operation in adverse weather conditions and at night, and therefore has singular tactical advantages over

Above:
Launch sequence of an AGM-65 Maverick air-to-surface missile from a General Dynamics F-16B Fighting Falcon. *General Dynamics 30-80959*

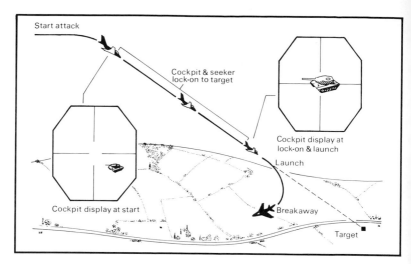

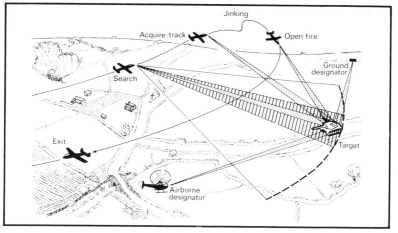

Typical attack sequence AGM-65A

Pave Penny attack scenario
The AAS-38 Pave Penny laser seeker pad allows the A-10 to acquire targets designated by forward air controllers. Reflected radiation from the target is then detected by the pod and is indicated on the HUD. The pilot then manoeuvres into position for attack

the earlier models, especially in the European theatre. The type is known as the **Imaging Infra-Red Maverick** and uses a Hughes IR seeker designed for deployment in conjunction with FLIR (Forward-Looking Infra-Red) systems, or with the LANTIRN (Low-Altitude Navigation and Targeting Infra-Red for Night) pod. This is carried by Fairchild Republic A-10 Thunderbolt II battlefield and anti-tank aircraft and General Dynamics F-16 Fighting Falcon fighters in the European theatre, or with the APR-38 radar-warning system of aircraft such as the McDonnell Douglas F-4 Phantom II 'Wild Weasel II' defence-suppression fighter. The AGM-65D is one of the most expensive Maverick variants, but with exceptional range and target-acquisition capabilities is of considerable value for the destruction of high-value targets.

The **AGM-65E Maverick** or **Laser Maverick** was introduced in 1985 as successor to the cancelled AGM-65C, and is fitted with the digitally-processed and less-costly Hughes tri-service laser seeker, as well as a more powerful 300lb (136.1kg) warhead with impact or delay fuses. The accuracy of the AGM-65E (and of the AGM-65F) is less than 5ft (1.5m), and the main operating service is the US Marine Corps.

The **AGM-65F Maverick** is the **Navy Maverick** version for the US Navy combining the airframe and imaging infra-red guidance of the AGM-65D with the 250lb (113kg) Mk 19 blast fragmentation warhead and fuse of the AGM-65E, plus a number of software changes to optimise the weapon's capabilities against warship targets. The tactical aircraft most often associated with this variant is the McDonnell Douglas F/A-18 Hornet and Grumman A-6 Intruder.

The **AGM-65G Maverick** is the US Air Force equivalent of the AGM-65F with the 300lb (136.1kg) warhead, and is designed for the destruction of hardened targets such as aircraft shelters and bunkers, though retaining a capability against tanks. The variant also introduces pneumatic control-actuation and a digital autopilot, reducing the cost of this important missile. Other features are a tracking mode that allows the operator, before launching the missile, to choose the area of a large target which the AGM-65G should strike, and a low-altitude trajectory to minimise the possibility of the guidance breaking lock in cloud. It has also been suggested that the type will be further developed with a small tactical nuclear (fission) warhead, the need for such a weapon having been expressed by the US Air Force as long ago as 1976.

USA

BOEING AGM-69A SRAM

Type: air-to-surface missile
Dimensions: diameter 17.5in (0.445m); length 168.0in (4.267m) for internal carriage, or 190.0in (4.826m) for external carriage with an aerodynamic tail fairing; span about 30.0in (762mm), given that the three fins are disposed at 120° to each other round the tail with each tip 15.0in (381mm) from the centreline
Weight: total round 2,240lb (1016.1kg)
Warhead: 300lb (136kg) 170/200kT W69 nuclear
Powerplant: one Lockheed SR75-LP-1 two-stage solid propellant rocket
Performance: speed Mach 2.8 to 3.2; range 100/137.5 miles (160.9/221.3km) from a high-altitude launch declining to 35/50 miles (56.3/80.5km) from a low-altitude launch
Guidance: Singer-Kearfott KT-76 inertial plus terrain-avoidance radar altimeter

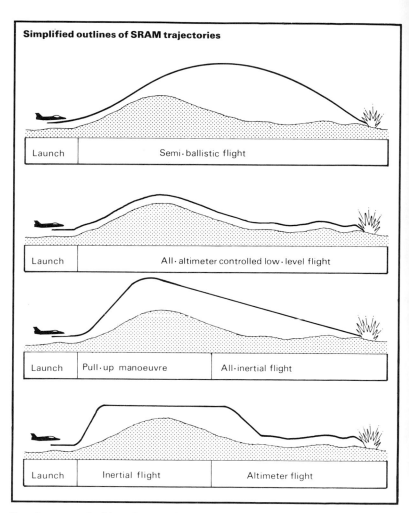

Simplified outlines of SRAM trajectories

| Launch | Semi·ballistic flight |

| Launch | All·altimeter controlled low·level flight |

| Launch | Pull·up manoeuvre | All·inertial flight |

| Launch | Inertial flight | Altimeter flight |

Development of a Short-Range Attack Missile was begun in the late 1950s, and the decade's advances in electronics and warhead miniaturisation are reflected in the fact that the missile was designed for carriage by fighters. But the current **Boeing AGM-69A SRAM** entered design in 1963 to give larger aircraft a useful stand-off capability against heavily-defended targets. The SRAM has exceptionally clean lines, without wings as its hypersonic flight performance allows the type to use body lift, but with three low-aspect-ratio tail surfaces indexed at 120° to each other. The SRAM entered service in 1972 as part of the primary armament for Boeing B-52 Stratofortress heavy bombers (20 SRAMs or eight SRAMs and four free-fall nuclear weapons) and General Dynamics FB-111 medium bombers (six SRAMs or two SRAMs and four free-fall nuclear weapons) as replacement for the North American

AGM-28 Hound Dog stand-off missile. The task planned for the weapon was stand-off attack against primary installations, but the AGM-69A is now tasked with defence-suppression tasks paving the way for AGM-86B air-launched cruise missiles and the delivery of gravity nuclear weapons. The SRAM has four basic attack profiles: semi-ballistic from launch to impact; altimeter-controlled terrain-following; ballistic pop-up from screening features followed by terrain-following; and combined terrain-following and inertial. Any of these profiles can include pre-programmed 180° course changes, and the warhead can be set for ground- or air-burst. The accuracy of the AGM-69A is classified, a figure of 500yd (457m) often being quoted, though an alternative claim of 100yd (91.4m) may be more realistic. Surviving missiles are being re-engined with a new Thiokol liquid propellant rocket developed for the upgraded AGM-69B variant that was cancelled in 1977. Since the proposed advent of the SRAM II, the baseline missile has frequently been designated **SRAM-A**.

In December 1986 Boeing was selected to develop a new SRAM missile instead of the proposed Advanced Strategic Air-Launched Missile. The **AGM-131A SRAM II** is schemed as a missile only, about two-thirds the size of the SRAM-A and using a composite-construction airframe (for low-observable or 'stealth' capability) as well as a laser ring-gyro inertial navigation system based on the new Very High Speed Integrated Circuit technology. The SRAM II will have an advanced two-pulse solid propellant rocket engine, and the 150/175kT thermonuclear warhead will have capability against hardened defence targets in advance of manned penetration bombers. The B-1B will be able to carry 20 SRAM IIs internally on the Common Strategic Rotary Launcher, and the Northrop B-2 will also carry the type. The SRAM II is due to enter service in 1992.

USA

GENERAL DYNAMICS AGM-78B STANDARD ARM

Type: air-to-surface anti-radiation missile
Dimensions: diameter 13.5in (0.343m); length 180.0in (4.572m); span 43.0in (1.092m)
Weight: total round 1,356lb (615.1kg)
Warhead: 214.7lb (97.4kg) blast fragmentation
Powerplant: one Aerojet Mk 27 Mod 4 dual-thrust solid propellant rocket
Performance: speed Mach 2.5; range varies with launch altitude and speed to a maximum of 56 miles (90km)
Guidance: Maxson Electronics passive radiation seeking

Derived from the RIM-66 Standard surface-to-air missile (and thus featuring the same configuration, with very low-aspect-ratio cruciform wings trailed by larger-span control surfaces indexed in line with the wings), the **General Dynamics AGM-78A Standard ARM** was introduced by the US Navy in 1968 as a longer-range complement to the AGM-45A Shrike. Like its predecessor, this initial variant uses the same no-memory Texas Instruments seeker with its attendant tactical limitations (loss of target and resultant ballistic trajectory) if the hostile radar is shut down.

The **AGM-78B Standard ARM** is a vastly developed model with a gimballed broadband seeker plus memory. The seeker requires no tuning before launch, thereby making it possible to engage targets of opportunity, and keeps the missile on its committed course even if the emitter shuts down. The missile achieves its best results with naval aircraft carrying the TIAS (Target Identification and Identification System) and with the US Air Force's McDonnell Douglas F-4GF 'Wild Weasel' defence-suppression aircraft, whose APR-38 emitter-location system can fulfil the same role as the TIAS in supplying the seeker head with emitter information up to the moment of launch.

The **AGM-78C Standard ARM** is a proposed version of the AGM-78B for the US Air Force and US Navy with a number of upgraded features. Some AGM-78A and AGM-78B missiles have been improved to this standard with field modification kits. The **AGM-78D Standard ARM** was another proposed version (together with a **AGM-78D2** subvariant) powered by the Mk 69 Model 0 solid propellant rocket and marked by further improvement of seeker capabilities.

USA

BOEING AGM-86B

Type: air-launched cruise missile
Dimensions: diameter 27.3in (0.693m); length 249.0in (6.325m); span 144.0in (3.658m)
Weight: total round 3,200lb (1,451.5kg)
Warhead: 200kT W80 Mod 1 thermonuclear
Propulsion: one 600lb (272kg) thrust Williams Research F107-WR-101 turbofan
Performance: speed 500mph (805km/hr); range 1,550 miles (2,495km)
Guidance: Litton P-1000 inertial with McDonnell Douglas DPW-23 TERCOM (TERrain COntour Matching) update

Entering service in 1981, the **Boeing AGM-86B** air-launched cruise missile is one of the US Air Force's most important strategic weapons, and is an aeroplane-configured missile with wings and tail surfaces that open from the basically triangular fuselage once the missile has been launched. The small turbofan is located in the tail, and is aspirated through a dorsal inlet that also deploys only after the missile has been launched. The core of the weapon is its exceptional guidance package; the inertial navigation system is updated in the missile's terminal flight stages by the TERCOM system that matches radar images of overflown terrain features with images pre-loaded into the computer memory to measure and correct angular deviation from course. About 170 Boeing B-52G bombers have been revised to carry 12 such weapons apiece (six on each of two underwing stations), plus four AGM-69A SRAMs and four free-fall nuclear weapons in the bomb bay. And 95 B-52H bombers have been reworked to the same standard, with provision on the latter for the carriage in the weapons bay of the Common Strategic Rotary Launcher for eight AGM-86B and/or AGM-69A SRAM missiles. The AGM-86s are designed for use against strategic targets, with the SRAMs available for defence suppression should the bombers have to penetrate defended airspace. The new Rockwell B-1B supersonic penetration bomber can carry eight AGM-86Bs on a rotary launcher in the weapons bay, plus another 14 under the wings. Though 4,348 AGM-86Bs were planned, only 1,715 have been built as newer cruise missiles (of the Convair ACM type) are planned for maintenance of US capability against a strengthened Soviet defence against air-launched cruise missiles. From 1985 in-service rounds have been retrofitted with an ECM package to improve their capabilities against the Soviet defences.

USA

TEXAS INSTRUMENTS AGM-88A HARM

Type: air-to-surface anti-radiation missile
Dimensions: diameter 10.0in (0.254m); length 164.2in (4.171m); span 44.0in (1.118m)
Weight: total round 796lb (361.1kg)
Warhead: 145lb (65.8kg) blast fragmentation
Powerplant: one Thiokol/Hercules YSR113-TC-1 solid propellant rocket
Performance: speed Mach 3+; range 46+ miles (74+km)
Guidance: Texas Instruments passive radiation seeking

Below:
The McDonnell Douglas F-4G Phantom II is the mainstay of the US Air Force's 'Wild Weasel' defence-suppression effort, the internal APR-38 radar-location system being complemented by missiles such as this General Dynamics AGM-78A Standard ARM, which offers exceptional capabilities counterbalanced to a certain extent by the missile's great weight and considerable cost. *USAF 80-269-1834*

Above:
Carried by attack aircraft such as this Grumman A-6E Intruder, the Texas Instruments AGM-88A HARM provides a combined offensive and defensive capability by giving the attacker the chance to deal with the radars that control the defences he must overfly en route to the target. *Grumman 832754*

The **Texas Instruments AGM-88A HARM** (High-speed Anti-Radiation Missile) began to enter US service in 1983 as successor to the tactically-limited AGM-45 Shrike and the costly (and also weighty) AGM-78 Standard ARM. The HARM is still a large weapon, with a long cylindrical body, a cruciform of cropped double-delta control surfaces at the mid-point, and a cruciform of fixed low-aspect-ratio fins at the rear, indexed in line with the control surfaces. The type offers good passive radiation homing with detection from the launch aircraft's sensor suite, in the form of the Itek ALR-45 or McDonnell Douglas APR-38 radar-warning receivers in US Air Force aircraft, and the AWG-25 equipment of the US Navy's Vought A-7 Corsair II. The missile's high speed also gives the hostile emitter minimum close-down time, and one of the HARM's greatest advantages over the Shrike is the use of a single broadband seeker rather than a choice of individually tailored seekers, making it possible for a single seeker to be used against the whole electronic range of land- and ship-based air-defence radars. Two other improvements are a continued homing capability even after the target emitter has been closed down (thanks to the incorporation of a memory in the guidance system) and software-controlled signal processing, giving the possibility of role expansion to cover additional radars. The HARM can be used in any of three modes: self-protection mode when the launch aircraft's radar-warning receiver detects a hostile emitter and programmes the missile before launch; pre-briefed mode with the missile fired blind towards a possible target with the seeker searching in flight and commanding a self-destruct if no target is discovered; and target-of-opportunity mode when the seeker of the unfired missile detects and locks on to an emitter.

USA

MOTOROLA AGM-122A SIDEARM

Type: air-to-surface anti-radiation missile
Dimensions: diameter 5.0in (0.127m); length 113.0in (2.871m); span 24.8in (0.63m)
Weight: total round 195lb (88.5kg)
Warhead: 10lb (4.54kg) blast fragmentation
Powerplant: one Rocketdyne Mk 36 Mod 2 solid propellant rocket
Performance: speed Mach 2.3; range 4,000yd (3,660m)
Guidance: Motorola passive radiation seeking

The **Motorola AGM-122A Sidearm** is currently entering service on US Marine Corps' Bell AH-1 SeaCobra attack helicopters and McDonnell Douglas/BAe AV-8 Harrier STOVL close-support aircraft. The Sidearm is a self-protection anti-radiation weapon for helicopters and light tactical aircraft, and is most notable for its light weight and comparatively low cost. The weapon is a conversion of the AIM-9C Sidewinder air-to-air missile, of which 885 have been held in storage for some years since the US Navy retired the Vought F-8 Crusader, the only aircraft to operate this sole semi-active radar homing version of the Sidewinder. The type is light and moderately advanced, but the seeker unit has to be cued before launch by the launch aircraft's radar homing and warning system.

EMERSON DEFENSE SYSTEMS AGM-123A SKIPPER II

Type: air-to-surface boosted glide bomb
Dimensions: diameter 14.0in (0.356m); length 169.0in (4.293m); span 63.0in (1.60m)
Weight: total round 1,283lb (582.0kg)
Warhead: 1,000lb (454kg) Mk 83 bomb
Powerplant: one Rocketdyne Mk 78 solid propellant rocket
Performance: speed transonic; range 34 miles (55km), limited in practice to 10.25 miles (16.5km)
Guidance: Texas Instruments semi-active laser homing

The **Emerson Defense Systems AGM-123A Skipper II** is a straightforward but thoroughly effective tactical weapon created by combining off-the-shelf components such as the Mk 83 1,000lb (454kg) general-purpose 'iron bomb', the rocket motor of the AGM-45B Shrike and a guidance/control system based on that of the 'Paveway III' series of guided bombs. The result is a highly accurate stand-off weapon with double the range of the 'Paveway' series. The weapon entered production in 1986, initially for US Navy aircraft such as the Grumman A-6 Intruder, Vought A-7 Corsair and McDonnell Douglas F/A-18 Hornet, and the manufacturer envisages the conversion of many current Paveway rounds to Skipper II standard.

NORTHROP AGM-136A 'TACIT RAINBOW'

Type: air-to-surface anti-radiation missile
Dimensions: diameter 14.0in (0.356m); length 100.0in (2.54m); span 69.4in (1.773m)
Weight: total round about 440lb (199.6kg)
Warhead: ?lb (?kg) blast fragmentation
Propulsion: one 240lb (109kg) thrust Williams International J400-WR-404 turbojet
Performance: speed 600mph (966km/hr); endurance 30min
Guidance: Texas Instruments passive radiation seeking

The result of a highly classified programme, the **Northrop AGM-136A 'Tacit Rainbow'** was revealed only in 1987. The prime contractor is Northrop, which used its BQM-74 Chukar target and reconnaissance drone as the aerodynamic and structural basis of this small and potentially decisive missile, whose flying surfaces deploy after launch. Support is provided by the Boeing Military Aircraft Co, Delco Systems Operations, Singer Kearfott Division, Texas Instruments and Williams International. The last indicates that this advanced anti-radar missile uses miniature jet propulsion, designed to secure longer range and/or extended loiter time. This loiter period allows the missile to use its endurance to search for ground-based emitters, whose locations are then stored in the memory of the missile's advanced guidance and homing package even if they are switched off. The missile can thus select the most important emitter and institute its terminal dive attack with considerable accuracy. The primary role of the 'Tacit Rainbow' missile is to clear the way for manned aircraft. Launched in front of the first wave of attack aircraft, the missile cruises over the intended attack route to select and attack an emitter associated with surface-to-air missiles or anti-aircraft artillery.

USA

ROCKWELL GBU-15

Type: air-to-surface glide bomb
Dimensions: diameter 18.0in (0.457m); length 155.0in (3.937m); span 59.0in (1.50m)
Weight: total round 2,515lb (1,140.8kg)
Warhead: 1,970lb (893.6kg) Mk 84 bomb (nominal weight, 2,000lb/907kg)
Powerplant: none
Performance: speed transonic; range between 1.5 and 80 miles (2.4 and 128.75km) depending on launch speed and altitude
Guidance: electro-optical homing for GBU-15(V)1/B and imaging infra-red homing for GBU-15(V)2/B

The **Rockwell HOBOS** (HOming BOmb System) was developed by Rockwell during the 1960s in parallel with the 'Paveway I' series of guided bombs, within the 'Pave Strike' programme, to give US aircraft the ability to hit pinpoint targets from stand-off ranges with modified 'iron' bombs. In comparison with the 'Paveway' series this **GBU-8** type uses electro-optical (TV) rather than laser guidance, at first with an image-contrast tracker and then with more advanced TV and infra-red seekers for enhanced nocturnal and adverse-weather capability. The three kits for the GBU-8 glide bombs are the image-contrast KMU-353A/B and KMU-390/B systems, and the infra-red KMU-359/B system. Each comprises a nose-mounted guidance section and, connected by strakes along the body of the bomb, a tail-mounted control section fitted with fins. The packages can be added to the 2,000lb (907kg) Mk 84 GP bomb (KMU-353A/B and KMU-359/B) and the 3,000lb (1,361kg) M118E1 demolition bomb (KMU-390/B). The accuracy of the system is 20ft (6.1m).

The **Rockwell GBU-15** is a much improved version of the HOBOS concept, developed on the basis of the **Modular Guided Weapon** (otherwise known as the **Cruciform Wing Weapon**) to extend stand-off range. The core weapon is the 2,000lb (907kg) Mk 84 bomb to which is fitted a guidance unit, a control package, a two-way data-link and a cruciform-wing aerodynamic kit. The guidance package of the **GBU-15(V)1/B** initial version is the daylight-only DSU-27A/B electro-optical type using the AXQ-14 data-link system, while that of the later **GBU-15(V)2/B** model is the all-weather day/night WGU-10/B imaging infra-red guidance of the AGM-65D Maverick. The guidance system allows the missile to be locked on to its target before or after launch, or alternatively for the weapon to be manually guided by the controller in the launch aircraft. Accuracy is in the order of 20ft (6.1m). A proposed development is the **GBU-15(V)N/B** with an SUU-54 dispenser (carrying 1,800 BLU-63 and/or BLU-86 anti-tank bomblets) as its payload, and guided by the electro-optical or imaging infra-red nose packages for attacks against airfields and armour, with secondary capability against motor transport and air-defence installations.

The **Rockwell AGM-130A** is a version of the GBU-15 weighing 2,917lb (1,323kg) with a Mk 84 bomb as payload, but in this instance powered by a strap-on Hercules solid propellant rocket for a range of 26,400yd (24,140m) from a low-altitude launch, thereby combining the full stand-off range capability of the GBU-15 series with all the tactical advantages of low-level penetration of defended airspace. The weapon has been redesignated somewhat, with a more cylindrical body, larger canards and smaller fins with control surfaces. The type has mid-course altitude and heading hold, and the terminal guidance system uses the same type of data-linked electro-optical or imaging infra-red system as does the GBU-15. The weapon's principal dimensions are similar to those of the GBU-15 apart from a length of 154.5in (3.924m). The role of the missile is low-altitude stand-off attack against heavily-defended targets, and the weapon has the same basic launch qualifications and targeting options as the GBU-15. The direct-attack mode is used when the guidance system can be locked on to the target before the missile is released, allowing a line-of-sight approach to the target, while the indirect-attack mode is used when the target cannot be locked into the guidance system before missile launch. In this latter mode the weapon glides down to a preset height of 2,000, 1,000 or 600ft (610, 305 or 185m) as a search is made for the target; during the mid-course phase missile height can be decreased by the operator in steps of 200ft (60m). Some 30sec after missile launch the motor is ignited, being jettisoned after it has burned out. The final approach to the target may be made with the seeker locked on to the target, or under manual control of the data-linked operator in the launch aircraft.

Developments of the AGM-130A are the **AGM-130B** airfield-attack version carrying as its warhead an SUU-54 (15 BLU-106/B Boosted Kinetic-Energy Penetrator and 75 British-designed Hunting HB876 area-denial submunitions) and having an overall weight of 2,560lb (1,161.2kg); and the **AGM-130C** hard-target version carrying as its payload the BLU-109/B Improved 2,000lb Warhead for decisive effect on hardened point targets.

TEXAS INSTRUMENTS 'PAVEWAY'/KMU-351A/B

Type: air-to-surface glide bomb
Dimensions: see below
Weight: total round 2,100lb (952.6kg)
Warhead: 1,970lb (893.6kg) Mk 84 bomb (nominal weight 2,000lb/
907kg)
Powerplant: none
Performance: speed transonic; range between 1,650 and 20,000yd
(1,510 and 18,200m) depending on launch speed and altitude
Guidance: semi-active laser homing

Introduced in 1967 after the first release of a laser-guided development weapon in 1965, the **Texas Instruments 'Paveway I'** family comprises a series of add-on laser-homing kits (marked-target seekers and associated control surfaces), weighing about 30lb (13.6kg) and designed for addition to standard low-drag general-purpose bombs to increase bombing accuracy against point targets when used in conjunction with an air- or ground-based laser designator. The kits are the KMU-342/B used with the 750lb (340kg) M117 demolition bomb; the KMU-351A/B used with the 2,000lb (907kg) Mk 84 general-purpose bomb; the KMU-370B/B used with the 3,000lb (1,361kg) M118E1 demolition bomb; the KMU-388A/B used with the 500lb (227kg) Mk 82 general-purpose bomb; the KMU-420/B used with the 500lb (227kg) Rockeye Mk 20 Mod 2 cluster bomb with 358 1.1lb/0.5kg anti-tank bomblets; and the KMU-421B used with the 2,000lb (907kg) SUU-54B cluster bomb. The advantage of the system is that the launch aircraft needs no modification and, unless it is the laser-designator platform, can depart from the target area. The system works in all visibility conditions, and the minimum cloud base for successful operation is 2,500ft (760m). The airborne designators most commonly associated with the series are the AVQ-26 'Pave Tack', AVQ-23 'Pave Spike' and LANTIRN (Low-Altitude Navigation and Targeting Infra-Red for Night) podded systems carried by many US aircraft. And any aircraft capable of lifting the baseline 'iron' bomb can deliver the Paveway weapon against a target designated by a third party.

Entering service in 1980, the **'Paveway II'** is an improved series based on the same basic concept but with a simpler (thus cheaper) guidance package and a folding wing aerofoil group added at the tail for extra manoeuvrability and enhanced cross-range capability. The weapons within this important basic designation are the **GBU-10E/B** and **GBU-10F/B** based on the 2,000lb (907kg) Mk 84 general-purpose bomb; the **GBU-12D/B** and **GBU-12F/B** based on the 500lb (227kg) Mk 82 general-purpose bomb; the **GBU-16B/B** and **GBU-16C/B** based on the 1,000lb (454kg) Mk 83 general-purpose bomb; and the **Mk 13/18UK** based on the British 1,000lb (454kg) Mk 13/18 general-purpose bomb. The GBU-10 has a diameter of 18.0in (0.457m) and a length of 169.9in (4.315m); and the GBU-12 has a diameter of 10.75in (0.273mm) and a length of 131.15in (3.331m).

Entering service in 1987, the **'Paveway III'** is an improved version of the

'Paveway II' with microprocessor controls and a digital autopilot intended for use primarily in the adverse weather and high-threat scenario of European operations. The 'Paveway III' is also designated the **Low-Level Laser-Guided Bomb**, and was designed for release at low level in either level flight or a zoom climb. It can, therefore, be fitted with high-lift folding wings, but can also be released at higher altitudes in dives as steep as 60°. The result is a weapon of far greater tactical flexibility than its predecessors. The variant fitted with the 2,000lb (907kg) Mk 84 general-purpose bomb as its warhead, has the service designation **GBU-24/B**. It also features an improved seeker and more advanced microprocessor technology, allowing low-level and off-axis stand-off delivery in conditions of low visibility, with mid-course guidance providing the possibility of delayed laser-designating and trajectory shaping. The primary data for the KBU-24 include a weight of 2,315lb (1,050.1kg), a length of 172.76in (4.388m) and spans of 36.0in (0.914m) folded and 81.6in (2.073m) open.

Left:
This General Dynamics F-111F is carrying four 'Paveway II' laser-guided bombs, the Ford AVQ-26 'Pave Tack' designating system package and an ALQ-119 electronic countermeasures pod. *General Dynamics 31-37864*

Below:
This 'Paveway II' laser-guided bomb is based on the Mk 84 general-purpose bomb, which can be seen as the core to which are attached the flip-open tail surfaces and the nose package complete with movable control surfaces and gimballed seeker head. *Rockwell 78-630-41*

Above:
The 'Paveway' kit can also be applied to the British 1,000lb (454kg) Mk 13/18 free-fall bomb for carriage by tactical aircraft such as this SEPECAT Jaguar GR Mk 1, which also sports a centreline drop tank and two electronic warfare pods (a Philips-Matra Phimat chaff/flare dispenser under the starboard wing and an ALQ-101 electronic countermeasures pod under the starboard wing). *BAe OP1507*

Below:
A SEPECAT Jaguar GR Mk 1 of No 6 Squadron from RAF Coltishall is seen with 1,000lb (454kg) 'iron' bombs under its fuselage and wings. *John Dunnell*

4: Anti-Ship Missiles

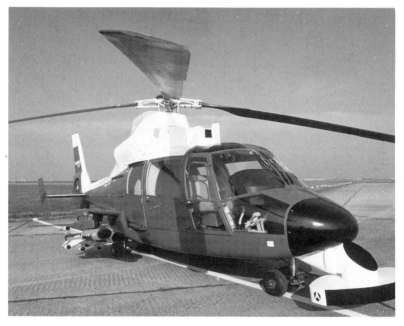

Above:
The Aérospatiale AS15TT lightweight anti-ship missile is carried in a quadruple installation on the Aérospatiale SA365F Dauphin 2 which also carries the associated Thomson-CSF Agrion 15 search and target-designation radar.
Aérospatiale

FRANCE

AÉROSPATIALE AS15TT

Type: helicopter-launched short range anti-ship missile
Dimensions: diameter 0.188m (7.40in); length 2.30m (90.55in); span 0.564m (22.2in)
Weight: total round 103kg (227.1lb)
Warhead: 29.7kg (65.5lb) blast fragmentation
Powerplant: one SNPE/Aérospatiale Anubis solid-propellant rocket
Performance: speed 1,000km/hr (621mph); range 16,000m (17,500yd)
Guidance: (height) Thomson-CSF autopilot designed to produce a reducing cruise altitude to a height determined by TRT radar altimeter, and (bearing) radar command

Entering service in the mid-1980s, the **Aérospatiale AS15TT** (Air-Sol 15 Tous Temps, or all-weather air-to-surface type 15) missile was financed mainly by Saudi Arabia. The result is a trim weapon of typical Aérospatiale configuration, with a tapered cylindrical body, a cruciform of swept delta wings on the mid-body, and a cruciform of slightly swept control surfaces at the tail and indexed in line with the wings. The missile was designed as successor to the AS12 as the primary weapon of ship- and shore-based light helicopters used against fast attack craft and other small naval units. The Aérospatiale SA365 Dauphin 2 and Aérospatiale SA332 Super Puma helicopters are the two major types currently qualified to operate the AS15TT. The missile is controlled in bearing by the helicopter's Thomson-CSF Agrion-15 radar, and in height by a programme that brings the missile down to sea-skimming height for the approach, and to wavetop height for the attack over the final 300m (985ft).

FRANCE

AÉROSPATIALE AM39 EXOCET

Type: air-launched medium range anti-ship missile
Dimensions: diameter 0.35m (13.75in); length 4.69m (184.65in); span 1.10m (43.31in)
Weight: total round 655kg (1,444.0lb)
Warhead: 165kg (363.75lb) GP1 blast fragmentation
Powerplant: one SNPE Condor solid propellant booster rocket and one SNPE Hélios solid propellant sustainer rocket
Performance: speed 1,140km/hr (708mph); range between 50 and 70km (31.1 and 43.5 miles) depending on launch speed and altitude
Guidance: inertial plus TRT RAM01 radar altimeter for mid-course phase, and EMD ADAC monopulse active radar for terminal phase

The most widely produced anti-ship missile of Western origins, the **Aérospatiale Exocet** was designed in the late 1960s originally as the MM38 ship-launched missile and began to enter service in 1974. Since that date the missile has been developed in several forms and seen extensive operational use, notably in the Anglo-Argentine Falklands War of 1982 and in the Iraqi-Iranian Gulf War. The missile's design is of standard Aérospatiale practice, with a cylindrical body plus tapered radome, a cruciform of mid-mounted swept delta wings, and an inline-indexed cruciform of slightly swept control surfaces at the tail. Development of the Exocet's air-launched version began in 1975, and the first round was test fired in December 1976 to allow service deliveries from July 1977. This initial **AM38 Exocet** was a limited-production helicopter-launched version of the MM38 using SNPE Epervier booster and SNPE Eole V sustainer rocket motors with concentric nozzles. A 1sec ignition delay was built into the booster to avoid damage to the launch platform.

The **AM39 Exocet** is the initial full-production air-launched version of the MM38 with a revised propulsion arrangement in a shorter body, reducing weight but increasing range. The missile is launched on range and bearing data provided by the launch aircraft's sensors and fire-control system, and cruises at low altitude until some 10,000m (10,935yd) from the missile's anticipated target, when the onboard X-band monopulse active seeker is activated. Once the target has been acquired the terminal phase is initiated at the lowest of three heights preselected at launch on the basis of sea state. The French launch platforms most commonly associated with the missile are the Aérospatiale SA321 Super Frelon helicopter, the Dassault-Breguet Atlantique 2 maritime patrol aircraft, the Dassault-Breguet Mirage F1E multi-role fighter and the Dassault-Breguet Super Etendard carrier-borne attack fighter. Late-production rounds have the Super ADAC homing radar, which offers the considerable tactical advantage of improving resistance to electronic countermeasures.

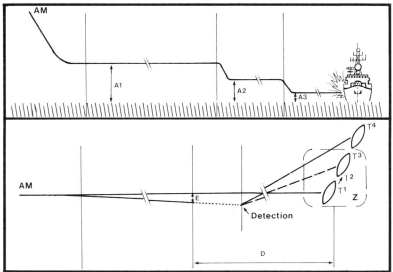

Aérospatiale AM39 Exocet – Vertical plane

AM   Missile freefalls 10m below launcher aircraft
Booster ignites, automatic guidance activated

A1   Missile is stabilised in direction of target at cruise altitude

A2   End of cruise phase. Missile descends to lower altitude

A3   Missile covers terminal approach phase at an altitude determined by sea conditions

●   The very short search phase which follows the activation of the seeker head can take place either at the end of the cruise phase, or during one or other of the approach phases, depending on the firing range

●   As a general rule, *A3* altitude guarantees impact on the target. However, should the missile overfly smaller target ships in rough sea conditions, the proximity fuse would detonate the explosive charge just above the deck

Aérospatiale AM39 Exocet – Horizontal plane

AM   Missile flies at *A1* altitude to a target position termed *T1*, designated at launch

E   The inertial platform maintains the missile on that course within a very small error

D   At a given distance from *T1*, the seeker is activated and sweeps a predetermined zone *Z* sufficient to compensate for any navigational or target designation errors

T3   Target detected at end of very short search phase. Exchange of data between seeker and inertial platform to determine movements of target, counter possible manoeuvres and choose best point of impact

AÉROSPATIALE/MBB ANS

Type: air-launched short/medium range anti-ship missile
Dimensions: diameter 0.35m (13.78in); length 5.70m (224.4in); span 1.10m (43.31in)
Weight: total round 950kg (2,094.4lb)
Warhead: 180kg (396.8lb) penetrating blast fragmentation
Powerplant: one MBB integral rocket-ramjet serving first as a solid propellant booster rocket and then as a rocket-ramjet sustainer
Performance: speed Mach 2 at sea level and Mach 3 at altitude; range 6/180+km (3.7/112+ miles)
Guidance: strapdown inertial for mid-course phase, and ESD Super ADAC active radar for terminal phase

The **Aérospatiale/MBB Anti-Navire Supersonique** (supersonic anti-ship) missile is currently under development for service in the early 1990s as successor to the Exocet and Kormoran air-launched missiles in French and West German service respectively. The ANS features a beautifully streamlined body with four very low-aspect-ratio wings on the mid-body, and a cruciform of tail controls indexed in line with the wings. The ANS has an advanced propulsion system, with an integral rocket for acceleration to Mach 2 cruising speed, at which it becomes a hybrid rocket ramjet with the rocket supplying fuel-rich gas to be mixed with liquid fuel for burning in the ramjet combustion chamber, which is aspirated through a quartet of inlets located round the leading edges of the wings. This contributes to a very high attack speed, which reduces the time available to the target for the implementation of countermeasures, and the terminal guidance will probably incorporate a home-on-jam mode. The type is also planned with exceptional electronic counter-countermeasures capability.

MBB KORMORAN

Type: air-launched medium range anti-ship missile
Dimensions: diameter 0.344m (13.54in); length 4.40m (173.23in); span 1.00m (39.37in)
Weight: total round 600kg (1,322.8lb)
Warhead: 165kg (363.8lb) radial blast fragmentation
Powerplant: two SNPE Pradès solid propellant booster rockets and one SNPE Eole IV solid-propellant sustainer rocket
Performance: speed 1,160km/hr (721mph); range 37km (23 miles)
Guidance: SFENA-Bodenseewerk strap-down inertial plus TRT radar altimeter for mid-course phase, and Thomson-CSF RE576 active/passive radar for terminal phase

Developed from the Nord AS 34 missile projected in France, the **MBB Kormoran** entered West German naval service in 1977 as the primary anti-ship weapon of Lockheed F-104G Starfighters operated by the Marineflieger; the weapon is now used on the Panavia Tornados operated by the same service and by the Italian Air Force. The missile has cylindrical body with tapered radome, a cruciform of highly swept mid-body delta wings and a cruciform of highly swept control fins indexed in line with the wings. After launch the Kormoran cruises at a height of 30m (100ft) to the approximate location of the target, then descends to wave-top height for the preset passive or active radar attack. The warhead is extremely potent, being designed to penetrate up to 90mm (3.54in) of metal on the ship's side before the 16 radially-disposed charges detonate to pierce the ship's bottom, decks and internal bulkheads.

The **Kormoran 2** is a much improved 630kg (1,389lb) weapon with a new, and considerably more compact, Thomson-CSF solid-state seeker with digital signal processing for higher hit probability and enhanced resistance to electronic countermeasures. The missile also possesses greater range and a 220kg (485lb) warhead of enhanced penetration capability. The Kormoran 2 is due to enter service on the Tornado in the late 1980s.

Below:
A Panavia Tornado IDS of the Italian Air Force is seen with an apparent load of six Kormoran anti-ship missiles. *Denis J. Calvert*

ISRAEL MILITARY INDUSTRIES
GABRIEL Mk 3A/S

Type: air-launched medium range anti-ship missile
Dimensions: diameter 0.34m (13.4in); length 3.84m (151.18in); span 1.10m (43.31in)
Weight: total round 558kg (1,230.2lb)
Warhead: 150kg (330.7lb) blast fragmentation
Powerplant: one solid-propellant rocket
Performance: speed transonic; range 40km (25 miles)
Guidance: intertial plus radar altimeter for mid-course phase, and active radar for terminal phase

Below:
In its air-launched form the IAI Gabriel Mk 3 offers Israeli attack aircraft a potent anti-ship capability using any of several guidance systems for maximum tactical flexibility. *Israel Aircraft Industries*

The **IMI Gabriel Mk 3A/S** is the air-launched version of the ship-launched Gabriel Mk 3, derived from the earlier Gabriel Mk 1 and 2 anti-ship missiles. The ship-launched Gabriel Mk 3 introduced a frequency-agile active radar seeker, through the optical and semi-active radar homing systems of the Gabriel Mk 1 and 2 can also be used to provide tactical flexibility and continued operability in face of electronic countermeasures. The weapon can have three guidance modes: fire-and-forget, fire-and-update via a data-link from a targeting helicopter, and fire-and-command using the launch vessel's radar. The missile cruises at 100m (330ft) and then descends to 20m (66ft) for the approach to the target, the attack phase being flown at a preset height of 1.5, 2.5 or 4m (4.9, 8.25 or 13.1ft) depending on the sea state. The Gabriel Mk 3A/S is the air-launched variant of this version with lighter weight, a slightly longer body and reduced-span wings all contributing to higher speed but reduced range.

The **Gabriel Mk 3A/S ER** is an extended range version of the Gabriel Mk 3A/S with a longer sustainer rocket that increases weight to 600kg (1,322.8lb) and range to 60km (37.3 miles), about that of the Gabriel Mk 3 variant.

An updated version planned for development in the late 1980s and early 1990s, with a length of 4.70m (185.04in) and powered by a small turbojet for a range of 200km (124 miles), will be designated the **Gabriel Mk 4**. This will probably have provision for mid-course update of its inertial navigation system.

ITALY

SISTEL SEA KILLER Mk 2

Type: helicopter-launched short/medium range anti-ship missile
Dimensions: diameter 0.206m (8.11in) for body, and 0.316m (12.44in) for warhead; length 4.832m (190.24in); span 0.978m (38.5in)
Weight: total round 340kg (749.6lb)
Warhead: 210kg (463lb) semi-armour-piercing blast fragmentation
Powerplant: one SEP 299 double-base solid propellant booster rocket and one SEP 300 composite solid propellant sustainer rocket
Performance: speed 1,080km/hr (671mph); range 25km (15.5 miles)
Guidance: combination of autopilot (azimuth) and radar altimeter (height) for mid-course phase, and SMA active radar for terminal phase

---

The **Sistel Sea Killer** is a lightweight anti-ship weapon, originally designed as the Sea Killer Mk 1 for use from fast attack craft. The **Sea Killer Mk 2** introduced a tandem-propulsion system for greater range with a larger warhead. The Sea Killer has a long and basically cylindrical body, two cruciform sets of marginally swept flying surfaces (a wider-span mid-body set and a narrower-span tail set) and a tandem booster of greater diameter than the main body and fitted with a cruciform of unswept fins.

The air-launched version of the Sea Killer Mk 2 is part of the Marte system, in which the missile is fired from a helicopter fitted with the SMA APQ-706 radar. Smaller helicopters such as the Agusta (Bell) AB.212ASW can carry one missile and the appropriate guidance equipment, but larger machines such as the Agusta (Sikorsky) ASH-3 can carry two missiles, the weight of the complete installation with two missiles being 1,165kg (2,568lb). The original **Marte Mk 1** system uses a simple development of the Sea Killer Mk 2 missile with the original parallel-section warhead weighing 70kg (154lb) within an overall missile weight of 300kg (661lb) and length of 4.70m (185.04in), complete with the booster stage; guidance over the maximum range of 20km (12.4 miles) is entrusted to a mixture of autopilot and radar altimeter for the mid-course phase, and Sistel radar beam-riding and/or optical guidance for the terminal phase. The **Marte Mk 2** system uses the improved Sea Killer Mk 2 described in the specification above. This has a revised warhead and guidance section based on that of the Otomat surface-launched anti-ship missile. The warhead weighs 210kg (463lb) including 60kg (132lb) of explosive, and the missile has active radar homing for 'fire-and-forget' operation. This improved Sea Killer Mk 2 is also planned as part of the armament fit for the Aeritalia/Aermacchi/EMBRAER AMX and Aermacchi MB339 fixed-wing light attack aircraft, though the higher speeds of these launch platforms allows the missile to be used without its booster stage.

NORWAY

KONGSBERG PENGUIN Mk 3

Type: air-launched medium range anti-ship missile
Dimensions: diameter 0.28m (11.02in); length 3.17m (124.8in); span 1.00m (39.37in)
Weight: total round 372kg (820.1lb)
Warhead: 121kg (267lb) semi-armour-piercing blast fragmentation
Powerplant: one Raufoss Ammunisjons/Atlantic Research Corporation solid propellant rocket
Performance: speed 1,100km/hr (684mph); range 60km (37.3 miles)
Guidance: Kongsberg Vapenfabrikk inertial for mid-course phase, and Kongsberg Vapenfabrikk infra-red homing for terminal phase

The **Kongsberg Penguin** was the Western world's first anti-ship missile, the original Penguin Mk 1 having been conceived in the early 1960s to enter service in 1972 as part of Norway's anti-invasion defences. This first model was optimised for use in the country's peculiar coastal waters after launch from fast attack craft and other small naval platforms. The result is a missile with infra-red terminal homing, treated as a round of ammunition and launched on information supplied by the launch platform's sensors and fire-control system. In configuration the missile is singular. The cylindrical body is conventional, with a rounded nose for the infra-red seeker, but the flying surfaces are unusual: the large swept wings are disposed in the standard cruciform fashion, at about the mid-body position, but have curved leading edges, and a similar planform is used for the canard control surfaces which are indexed in line with the wings but located on the extreme nose. The Penguin Mk 2 is an improved Mk 1 with range boosted to 30km (18.6 miles) and weight increased to 340kg (750lb) in the ship-launched Penguin Mk 2 Mod 3 variant. The type entered service in the early 1980s. The basic type has been further developed for air launch as the **Penguin Mk 2 Mod 7** (US designation **AGM-119B** for use with helicopters such as the Kaman SH-2F Seasprite and Sikorsky SH-60B Seahawk) with a weight of 385kg (848.8lb) and a length of 3.02m (118.9in). This variant includes a number of Penguin Mk 3 improvements, notably in the seeker and signal processor, and has a new two-stage rocket and fully digital electronics in place of the Mk 2 variants' analog electronics.

The **Penguin Mk 3** is an air-launched development intended primarily for the Royal Norwegian Air Force's General Dynamics F-16 Fighting Falcon multi-role fighters. The variant, which possesses the US designation **AGM-119A**, has a longer body, shorter-span wings, a single-stage rocket and a radar altimeter. The Penguin Mk 3 is a capable weapon programmed to fly a dogleg approach to the target via one or more waypoints after launch on the basis of radar information from the launch aircraft, or of visual sighting with data entered into the missile via the pilot's head-up display. As on earlier versions of the missile, the use of infra-red terminal homing, activated only when the missile has reached the target's anticipated position, give the target vessel virtually no warning of the missile's imminent arrival, so reducing the time available for countermeasures.

Below:
The air-launched Kongsberg Penguin Mk 3 is a versatile anti-ship missile. This cutaway illustration shows the launch adaptor with electrical connections (above) and the missile (below). From front to rear, the missile's main features are the infra-red sensor, canard foreplanes for control, radar altimeter, guidance electronics, inertial navigation unit, warhead, fuse, fixed wings with moving control surfaces, and the solid-propellant rocket motor.
A-S Kongsbergvåpenfabrikk 30065

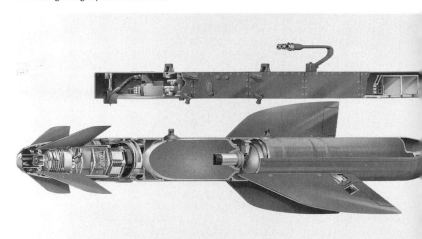

SAAB RB 04E

Type: air-launched medium range anti-ship missile
Dimensions: diameter 0.5m (19.69in); length 4.45m (175.2in); span 1.97m (77.56in)
Weight: total round 616kg (1,358.0lb)
Warhead: 300kg (661.4lb) blast fragmentation
Powerplant: one IMI Summerfield two-stage solid propellant rocket
Performance: speed high subsonic; range varies with launch speed and altitude to a maximum of 32km (19.9 miles)
Guidance: Saab two-axis autopilot for mid-course phase, and Philips Elektronikindustrier active radar for terminal phase

The **Saab RB 04** was the first European air-to-surface missile with active radar terminal homing, giving all-weather fire-and-forget capability. The weapon's development started in 1949, and ultimately led to one of the world's longest-running missile production programmes (1958-78). The type was planned as an anti-ship weapon, but has secondary capability against land targets. The layout of the RB 04 is unusual: large swept wings (with endplate vertical surfaces) at the rear and a cruciform arrangement of delta control surfaces (indexed in line with the wings) towards the nose. The **RB**

Below:
A Saab RB 04E hangs from its special adapter on one of a Saab Viggen's underfuselage hardpoints. *Saab-Scania/A. Anderson*

04C was the initial model, entering service in 1958, and spans 2.04m (80.31in). The RB 04 is carried by Sweden's Saab 35 Draken and Saab 37 Viggen attack aircraft.

The **RB 04D** is an improved model that entered service during the later 1960s with an upgraded rocket motor and modernised guidance, and the **RB 04E** is the final production version with wings of reduced span plus modernised guidance as well as an improved structure. Despite the age of the basic concept, this final variant is believed to have very advanced technical features even by current standards.

SWEDEN

SAAB RBS 15F

Type: air-launched medium/long range anti-ship missile
Dimensions: diameter 05m (19.69in); length 4.35m (171.26in); span
   1.4m (55.1in)
Weight: total round 598kg (1,318.3lb)
Warhead: ?kg (?lb) blast fragmentation
Powerplant: one 377kg (831lb) thrust Microturbo TRI 60-2 Model 007
   turbojet
Performance: speed high subsonic; range 150km (93.2 miles)
Guidance: pre-programmed autopilot plus radar altimeter for
   mid-course phase, and Philips Elektronikindustrier active radar for
   terminal phase

The **Saab RBS 15** is a highly capable anti-ship missile due to enter service in 1988 in its ship-launched RBS 15M variant with two solid propellant boosters. Development from 1982 has evolved the **RBS 15F** air-launched version, which has no requirement for the launch boosters, and is thus lighter and also longer ranged. The missile has a substantial body, a cruciform of aft-mounted delta wings, a cruciform of swept canard control surfaces indexed at 45° to the wings, and a ventral inlet for the fuel-economical turbojet between the lower pair of wings. After mid-course cruise at modest height, the active seeker is turned on and the missile descends to sea-skimming height for the attack. The particularly notable feature of the RBS 15F is its extremely advanced Philips seeker, which is frequency-agile, and has digital signal processing, a choice of search modes and patterns, variable electronic counter-countermeasures, and target-choice logic to allow the missile to choose the most important of several possible targets. The main launch platform is the Saab 37 Viggen multi-role aircraft.

BRITISH AEROSPACE SEA EAGLE

Type: air-launched medium/long range anti-ship missile
Dimensions: diameter 15.75in (0.40m); length 163.0in (4.14m); span
  47.3in (1.201m)
Weight: total round 1,325lb (601.0kg)
Warhead: 500lb (226.8kg) Royal Ordnance penetrating blast
  fragmentation
Powerplant: one 787lb (367kg) thrust Microturbo TRI 60-1 Model 067
  turbojet
Performance: speed 685+mph (1,102+km/hr); range 80 miles (130km)
  decreasing with lower launch altitude
Guidance: strapdown inertial plus Plessey radar altimeter for
  mid-course phase, and Marconi active radar for terminal phase

Below:
Launch of a BAe Sea Eagle from a BAe Sea Harrier FRS Mk 1 strike fighter.
BAe C3584/F

The **British Aerospace Sea Eagle** began to enter service in 1986 after development from 1976 as the P3T. The structural and aerodynamic basis of the weapon is the Martel air-to-surface missile but, in this longer range application, fitted with a turbojet aspirated through a ventral inlet located between the lower pair of the four mid-mounted swept delta wings, which are trailed by the inline-indexed control surfaces. The missile was designed mainly for aircraft launch platforms (the BAe Sea Harrier being able to carry two and the BAe Buccaneer four), and is notable for its good speed and range. The Sea Eagle has a thoroughly modern guidance system, the strapdown inertial portion having a microprocessor into which the launch platform loads data on the target's position, bearing, course and speed just before launching the Sea Eagle. The missile then cruises at low height, thereby reducing its chances of being spotted optically or electro-magnetically, and the active seeker is of an advanced type. The large warhead is effective against most naval targets. The basic missile has also been developed as the Sea Eagle SL (P5T) surface-launched version for use by coastal batteries or warships, fitted with a pair of jettisonable solid-propellant booster rockets of the type developed to provide the missile with helicopter-launch capability for the Indian Navy's Westland Advanced Sea King Mk 42s.

UK
_____

BRITISH AEROSPACE SEA SKUA

Type: air-launched short range anti-ship missile
Dimensions: diameter 9.75in (0.248m); length 98.5in (2.502m); span
    28.5in (0.724m)
Weight: total round 325lb (147.4kg)
Warhead: 44lb (20.0kg) Royal Ordnance blast fragmentation
Propulsion: one BAJ Vickers solid-propellant booster rocket and one
    BAJ Vickers solid-propellant sustainer rocket
Performance: speed more than 685mph (1,102km/hr); range 22,000yd
    (20,115m)
Guidance: strapdown inertial plus BAe/TRT radar altimeter for
    mid-course phase, and Marconi semi-active radar for terminal phase

The **British Aerospace Sea Skua** was pushed into early service as a result of the demands of the Anglo-Argentine Falklands War in 1982, and is a helicopter-launched anti-ship missile intended for the engagement of light and medium naval targets. Operational experience has combined with combat success to prove the missile an excellent weapon. The Sea Skua's accuracy and warhead are sufficient to ensure that small targets are sunk and medium targets crippled; the weapon's light weight and small size mean that it can be carried in useful numbers by helicopters such as the Westland Lynx, which can be fitted with four such missiles. In configuration the Sea Skua has a substantial forebody and a narrower cylindrical afterbody. The forebody contains the electronics, warhead and sustainer motor, the last exhausting through an arrangement of inlined lateral nozzles; the afterbody containing the booster and is surrounded by the cruciform of fixed and only slightly

Above:
Four BAe Sea Skua missiles on a Westland Lynx HAS Mk 2 light naval helicopter. *BAe C3163/B*

swept stabilising fins, which are indexed at 45° to the cruciform of moving swept delta wings on the forebody. The autopilot/altimeter cruise phase of the flight, an any one of the four preselected cruise altitudes, is followed by a rapid climb to the altitude at which the semi-active radar homing system can lock on to the reflections of the Ferranti Seaspray radar carried by the Lynx, though the adoption of other types as launch platforms will necessitate alterations to this system. The Sea Skua can also be launched on the basis of target and launcher information provided by electronic support measures and the Decca Tactical Air Navigation System, with the Seaspray illuminating radar activated only at the last minute to provide the target with minimum reaction time.

USA

McDONNELL DOUGLAS AGM-84A HARPOON

Type: air-launched medium range anti-ship missile
Dimensions: diameter 13.5in (0.343m); length 151.0in (3.835m); span
  36.0in (0.914m)
Weight: total round 1,160lb (526.2kg)
Warhead: 488lb (221.4kg) penetrating blast fragmentation
Powerplant: one 680lb (308kg) thrust Teledyne Continental
  J402-CA-400 turbojet
Performance: speed 645mph (1,038km/hr); range 68 miles (110km)
Guidance: Lear-Siegler or Northrop strapdown inertial plus Honeywell
  APN-194 radar altimeter for mid-course phase, and Texas
  Instruments PR-53/DSQ-58 two-axis active radar for terminal phase

The Western world's most important anti-ship missile, the **McDonnell Douglas Harpoon** was planned in the late 1960s as an advanced yet modestly priced weapon with emphasis on reliability rather than outright performance. The only exceptions to this stricture were the electronic capability and range, where the use of a turbojet rather than a rocket in the sustainer role pays handsome dividends. The Harpoon is based on a cylindrical body of large diameter, with fixed trapezoidal wings of modest sweep in the centrebody position, and moving control surfaces of similar shape in the aft position, indexed in line with the wings. The turbojet sustainer is aspirated via a flush ventral inlet between the lower pair of wings. The missile was first deployed during the mid-1970s in its RGM-84A ship-launched version with a jettisonable Aerojet booster rocket. This baseline missile can be fired in range and bearing mode, allowing the late activation of the active radar as a means of reducing the chances of the missile being detected through its own emissions, or in the bearing-only mode for earlier activation of the radar where the precise location of the target is not available at missile launch time. If no target is found after the low-level approach, the missile goes into a pre-programmed search pattern, and acquisition of the target is followed in the 57-mile (91.7km) range Block I missiles of the initial production batch by a steep climb and dive on to the target's upper surfaces. Currently in production is the Block II long range type

with range increased to more than 120 miles (193km), plus variable flight profiles and increased capability against electronic countermeasures. The **AGM-84A Harpoon** air-launched version needs no booster and is thus shorter and lighter than the RGM-84A.

The **AGM-84B Harpoon** is an air-launched version with a wholly sea-skimming flight profile without the pop-up feature of the AGM-84A, thus reducing the target's chances of spotting and countering the weapon. The **AGM-84C Harpoon** variant is improved in comparison with the earlier version, this air-launched model incorporating the pop-up and sea-skimming flight profiles of the AGM-84A and AGM-84B respectively. The model is entering service in the second half of the 1980s. The **AGM-84D Harpoon** is a longer range version that incorporates Block II range capabilities with improved electronic counter-countermeasures, and provision for the pre-programming of a dog-leg approach via three waypoints and for the selection of alternative terminal approaches.

Due to start trials in 1988, the **SLAM** (Stand-off Land-Attack Missile) is a derivative of the Harpoon for carriage by US Navy and US Marine Corps Grumman A-6 Intruder and McDonnell Douglas F/A-18 Hornet aircraft. The weapon combines the airframe, powerplant and warhead of the Harpoon with the imaging infra-red terminal guidance unit of the AGM-65D Maverick air-to-surface missile, the data-link of the AGM-62 Walleye glide bomb, and a Global Positioning System receiver.

Left:
In its attack guise the McDonnell Douglas F/A-18A Hornet can carry two McDonnell Douglas AGM-84A Harpoon anti-ship missiles without difficulty. *McDonnell Douglas C22-383-18*

Below:
Launch of a McDonnell Douglas AGM-84A Harpoon anti-ship missile from one of the port underwing hardpoints of a Lockheed P-3 Orion maritime patrol aeroplane. *US Navy*

5: Anti-Tank Missiles

FRANCE/WEST GERMANY

EUROMISSILE HOT

Type: helicopter-launched long range heavyweight anti-tank missile
Dimensions: diameter 0.165m (6.5in); length 1.275m (50.20in); span 0.312m (12.28in)
Weight: total around 23.5kg (51.8lb)
Warhead: 6kg (13.2lb) hollow-charge HE
Powerplant: one SNPE Bugéat solid-propellant booster rocket and one SNPE Infra solid-propellant sustainer rocket
Performance: speed 865km/hr (537mph); range 75/4,250m (82/4,650yd)
Guidance: SAT/Eltro wire semi-automatic command to line of sight

Entering service in the early 1970s, the **Euromissile HOT** (Haute subsonique Optiquement téléguidé tiré d'un Tube, or high-subsonic optically-guided tube-launched) missile is an extremely powerful anti-tank weapon designed originally for static ground use but rapidly evolved for installation also in armoured fighting vehicles and helicopters. The missile can be used in single or multiple tube launchers, and its 136mm (5.35in) diameter warhead, carrying 3kg (6.61lb) of explosives, can penetrate more than 800mm (31.5in) of armour under optimum conditions, though a more realistic figure is 280mm (11in) at a 65° impact angle. In configuration the missile has a wide cylindrical body to maximise the diameter of the all-important hollow-charge warhead. A cruciform of moderately swept wings springs open laterally as the missile emerges from its launch tube, and the exhausts for the booster rocket are disposed radially just behind the wings. The sustainer exhausts through the tail via jet deflectors that are used for control. The type's primary disadvantage is a modest speed: this means that it takes the missile about 17sec to reach its maximum range even when launched from a helicopter, which has to remain exposed (and thus vulnerable) for this time. The HOT's intermediate times are 8.7sec to 2,000m (2,185yd), 12.5sec to 3,000m (3,280yd) and 16.3sec to 4,000m (4,375yd). The stabilised sight generally associated with the HOT in the helicopters most frequently associated with the type (the Aérospatiale SA342 Gazelle and MBB BO105P) is the SFIM APX M397 unit, which is mounted as part of a gyro-stabilised unit in the roof of the launch helicopter.

The **HOT 2** is an improved and updated version of the baseline weapon, introduced to service in 1985 and featuring much-enhanced armour penetration as a result of its larger 150mm (5.9in) diameter warhead, containing 4.1kg (9lb) of explosive. The HOT 2 is also faster than its predecessor, with consequent tactical advantages. Further improvement in capability will be provided by adoption of the stabilised Viviane day/night sight currently entering service: this provides a genuine nocturnal capability, and the West Germans are developing a similar capability with the integration of a FLIR sight with the HOT system.

BOFORS RBS 56 BILL

Type: helicopter-launched medium range anti-tank missile
Dimensions: diameter 0.15m (5.91in); length 0.90m (35.43in); span
0.41m (16.14in)
Weight: total round 10.7kg (23.59lb)
Warhead: ?kg (?lb) hollow-charge HE
Powerplant: one Royal Ordnance dual-thrust solid-propellant rocket
Performance: speed 720km/hr (447mph); range 150/2,000m
(165/2,185yd)
Guidance: wire semi-automatic command to line of sight

Entering service in the later 1980s, the **Bofors RBS 56 Bill** (pick) is a highly
advanced anti-tank missile fired, in its basic ground-launched application,
from a container tube fitted with a sight unit and mounted on a tripod. In the
helicopter-launched application the missile container, which is delivered
complete with the missile as a certified round of ammunition weighing
20.5kg (45.2lb), can be fitted to the outside of a helicopter in the standard
fashion for such weapons. The keys to the Bill's capabilities are its guidance
system, which flies the missile 1.0m (39.4in) above the operator's line of
sight, and its combination of proximity fuse and shaped-charge warhead,
which is angled to fire downwards and forwards at −30° from the missile
centreline as the weapon overflies the target's most vulnerable upper
surfaces. This means that the jet of gas and vaporised metal formed by the
warhead's detonation strikes and burns through the target tank's thinnest
armour. The warhead and fuse are located in the centre of the wide-diameter
missile, just forward of the cruciform of high aspect-ratio wings, designed to
spring open as the missile emerged from the launch tube; control is effected
by a smaller cruciform of spring open swept tail surfaces indexed at 45° to
the wings. The rocket motor is located in the extreme nose, exhausting
through four radially-disposed nozzles just forward of the warhead section.
The missile's flight times are 6sec to 1,200m (1,315yd) and 11sec to 2,000m
(2,185yd). In common with other anti-tank missiles, the RBS 56 had greater
capability against stationary targets, but the tactical realities of the modern
battlefield were not forgotten in the design and the RBS 56 can thus engage
crossing targets, moving at a maximum speed of 36km/hr (22mph), at range
of between 300 and 2,000m (330 and 2,185yd).

HUGHES BGM-71A TOW

Type: helicopter-launched medium/long range heavyweight anti-tank missile

Dimensions: diameter 6.0in (0.152m); length 46.25in (1.174m); span 13.5in (0.343m)

Weight: total round 49.6lb (22.5kg)

Warhead: 8.6lb (3.9kg) Picatinny Arsenal hollow-charge HE

Powerplant: one Hercules K41 two-stage solid-propellant rocket

Performance: 700mph (1,127km/hr); range (pre-1976 models) 70/3,280yd (65/3,000m) or (post-1976 models) 70/4,100yd (65/3,750m)

Guidance: Emerson Electric wire semi-automatic command to line of sight

Entering service in 1970, the Hughes **BGM-71A TOW** (Tube-launched Optically-tracked Wire-guided) missile is without doubt the West's most important anti-tank weapon. The TOW is a heavyweight missile designed for vehicle- or helicopter-borne launchers, and has proved its capabilities in several wars. The layout includes flick-out cruciforms of high-aspect-ratio flight surfaces (fixed centre-body wings and moving aft-body control fins indexed at 45° to the wings), and aft-mounted booster rocket, a centrally-mounted sustainer rocket exhausting through four oblique nozzles between the wings, and in the nose the warhead. This last contains 5.3lb (2.4kg) of explosive, and has shown itself able to penetrate 600mm (23.6in) of armour under normal operational conditions. The range of this initial model is limited to 3,280yd (3,000m) by the length of its guidance wires. **BGM-71B Extended-Range TOW** is the semi-official designation of the basic weapon produced from 1976 with greater range than the original model as the result of the lengthening of the guidance wires to 4,100yd (3,750m).

Below:
The Bell AH-1S is the latest version of the single-engined HueyCobra for land service, and is seen here in anti-tank configuration with eight Hughes BGM-71 TOW missiles used with the sight system in the trainable nose turret.
Bell-Textron 027593

Introduced in the early 1980s in response to the development of Soviet tanks with improved armour, the **BGM-71C Improved TOW** is an interim model that features a larger-diameter 5in (0.127m) warhead with LX-14 explosive and a telescoping 15in (0.381m) nose probe that extends in flight to ensure a perfect stand-off distance for the detonation of the shaped-charge warhead. This model has a length of 70.0in (1.778m) with the probe extended, and weighs 56.65lb (25.7kg). Armour penetration with the new warhead increases to 700mm (27.6in).

Introduced in 1983 as the standard US weapon for tackling the latest Soviet tanks at long range, the **BGM-71D TOW 2** has an improved double-base motor (offering about 30% greater impulse) and a 13.2lb (6kg) warhead increased in diameter to 6in (0.152m) and provided with a 21.25in (0.564m) nose probe ensuring optimum stand-off distance for penetration of 800mm (31.5in) of armour. This significant variant weighs 61.95lb (28.1kg) and, though it can be fired from the original analog-electronics launcher, it is designed for use with an improved digital-electronics launcher fitted with thermal as well as optical sights, and with a more advanced guidance package.

Hughes has also proposed four developments of this powerful weapon with the provisional designations **TOW 2A** (a variant with an improved direct-attack warhead), **TOW 2B** (a top-attack version with a millimetre-wave radar or electro-optical fuse), **TOW 2D** (of which no details have been released), and **TOW 2N** (with wire-less command system of unspecified type, supersonic speed and a range of 10,000yd/9,145m). Tested in 1987 was the TOW 2A variant, which has a small explosive charge on its nose probe; this is designed to trigger the target's reactive armour, so removing the explosive obstacle to the main warhead's gas/metal vapour jet. Though the system works in its basic elements, its operational utility is doubtful because operators have found it very difficult to control the nose-heavy missile. Israel Aircraft Industries has produced a missile based on the TOW, and this **IAI Mapats** uses unjammable laser beam-rising guidance for extreme accuracy and range out to 10,000m (10,935yd).

ROCKWELL AGM-114A HELLFIRE

Type: air-to-surface anti-tank heavyweight missile
Dimensions: diameter 7.0in (0.178m); length 64.0in (1.626m); span 13.0in (0.33m)
Weight: total round 98.86lb (44.84kg)
Warhead: 20lb (9.1kg) hollow-charge HE
Propulsion: one Thiokol TX-657 solid-propellant rocket
Performance: speed high subsonic; range 6,500yd (5,945m)
Guidance: autopilot for mid-course phase, and Martin Marietta semi-active laser homing for the terminal phase

The **Rockwell AGM-114A Hellfire** (heliborne-launched fire-and-forget) missile is an impressive weapon that opens up the possibility of fire-and-forget helicopter attacks against armoured formations, the missile

Hellfire indirect launch

An expensive aircraft such as the AH-64 Apache will attempt to keep well back from hostile defences. Rather than go looking for targets, whenever possible it will fire against ones already located and designated by ground or airborne laser illuminators

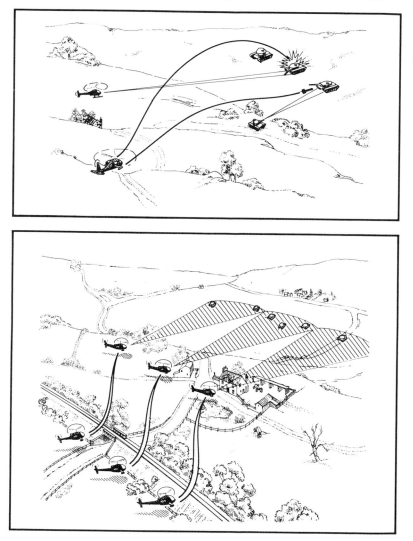

Ambush positions

In combat, the Apache will attempt to move forward to secondary hiding places. When targets are within range the aircraft will take up its final ambush position then launch its missiles. In the same fashion as a tank, the Apache will fire several rounds then withdraw to a new ambush position

Currently the ultimate battlefield helicopter, the McDonnell Douglas Helicopters AH-64A Apache has an extremely capable (and expensive) electronics suite, and its armament includes an underfuselage 30mm McDonnell Douglas M230 cannon and up to 16 (though only eight are being carried here) Rockwell AGM-114A Hellfire laser-guided missiles.
McDonnell Douglas

having proved itself able to home on the reflections of tanks laser-illuminated by either aerial or ground-based designators. The target need not be illuminated before the missile has been launched, at a stroke reducing the time the target has to undertake defensive measures and also reducing the launch platform's vulnerability to countermeasures. Indeed, the helicopter need not rise from cover and acquire the target at all, it being possible to fire the missile completely blind, allowing it to acquire its target (illuminated by a third party) late in its flight. The configuration of the missile is conditioned largely by the diameter of the warhead, which has to be as large as possible for optimum hollow-charge effect. This results in a portly missile with a cruciform of low-aspect-ratio aft-mounted wings and four trapezoidal control canards indexed in line with the wings. The weapon was developed as the US Army's HMMS (Hellfire Modular Missile System), and Rockwell is now looking at advanced versions of the missile. In the short term possible developments are 'hardening' of the seeker section to provide greater resistance to countermeasures, and a pulse rocket propulsion system to boost range by as much as 50%. In the longer term Rockwell is working with Marconi Defence Systems of the UK towards a derivative with millimetre-wave active radar guidance. This would be particularly useful on European battlefields as it offers all-weather capability as well as the possibility of fire-and-forget rapid reaction, covert launch capability, seek-and-destroy capability with lock-on only after launch, all-aspect attack capability, and greater capability for multiple target engagements.

The **AGM-114B Hellfire** is the AGM-114A version for the US Navy and US Marine Corps with a different motor and homing guidance provided by a choice of three different seeker modules. The **AGM-114C Hellfire** is the US Army version of the AGM-114B without the safe-arm feature required for US Navy shipboard storage.

6: Rockets

BELGIUM

FORGES de ZEEBRUGGE 2.75in FFAR

Type: air-to-surface and air-to-air rocket
Dimensions: diameter 2.75in (0.6985m); length 46.85in (1.19m); fin
  span 10.0in (0.254m)
Weight: 8.6 to 11.9kg (18.96 to 26.23lb) depending on warhead type
Warhead: varies between 2.9 and 6.2kg (6.4 and 13.7lb) depending on
  type
Powerplant: one solid-propellant rocket
Performance: range 500/6,000m (545/6,560yd) for Mk 4 and Mk 40
  types, 500/8,800m (545/9,625yd) for FZ-67 and FZ-68 types, and
  500/9,000m (545/9,845yd) for NRZ-96 type

Below:
**The McDonnell Douglas F-4E Phantom II multi-role fighter can carry an
enormous diversity of weapon types, the close-support task being handled
with a combination such as that seen here: free-fall bombs and four 19-tube
LAU-series launchers for 2.75in (70mm) FFAR rockets.**
McDonnell Douglas D4C-7974

The **Forges de Zeebrugge 2.75in FFAR** (Folding-Fin Aircraft Rocket) is a very widely used tactical weapon with four folding tail fins, originally developed in the USA as the 'Mighty Mouse' series in the air-to-air role with a 6lb (2.7kg) warhead, developing in the 1960s to a 10lb (4.54kg) warhead and ultimately to a 17lb (7.7kg) type. The rocket has been produced in huge numbers by American and overseas contractors, but since 1958 the Belgian company Les Forges de Zeebrugge has been the main supplier of FFAR weapons, and has developed the type into a highly capable air-to-surface type with a number of motors and warheads. The motor of the original Mk 4 and Mk 40 versions had 5.75lb (2.6kg) of propellant and offered quite a low thrust for between 1.2 and 1.4sec, providing the rocket with adequate range but leaving it highly susceptible to gravity and crosswind effects. Then the FZ-67 and FZ-68 motors, with 0.8 and 0.9sec burns, were developed from the US Mk 66 type to provide higher specific thrust with all the advantages this offered in terms of range and comparative immunity to gravity and crosswind. The latest NRZ-96 motor (used in the air- and surface-launched FFAR) was developed in conjunction with the French company SNPE, and is 5.7kg (12.6lb) in weight with 3kg (6.6lb) of composite propellant, and is 1.03m (40.55in) in length. The external motor shape remains unaltered, allowing the existing fin assembly and warhead types to be added, but its higher thrust and longer burn provide greater velocity. Other advantages are improved accuracy and greater payload in the form of heavier warheads. There are 10 main warhead types associated with the Forges de Zeebrugge rockets, giving the type very operational flexibility.

Below:
Rockets can give a useful ground-attack capability to light aircraft such as this Pilatus PC-7, generally used as a trainer but capable of undertaking the light attack role with armament including four launchers for 70mm (2.75in) Forges de Zeebrugge rockets and twin Fabrique Nationale gun pods each carrying two 7.62mm (0.3in) machine guns. *SA / or Forges de Zeebrugge*

CANADA

BRISTOL AEROSPACE CRV7

Type: air-to-surface and air-to-air rocket
Dimensions: diameter 2.75in (0.6985m); length 41.0in (1.041m)
without warhead
Weight: round excluding warhead 14.55lb (6.6kg)
Warhead: varies depending on specific type (see below)
Powerplant: one composite solid-propellant rocket in the form of
either the C14 for use on rockets carried by fixed-wing aircraft, or the
C15 designed for use on rockets carried by helicopters
Performance: speed 2,800 or 3,350mph (4,506 or 5,391km/hr) with a 10
or 8lb (4.5 or 3.3kg) warhead after launch from an aircraft flying at
620mph (998km/hr); range typically 7,100yd (6,490m) in the
air-to-surface role

The **Bristol Aerospace CRV7** is a Canadian unguided rocket designed for
total compatibility with the 2.75in (0.6985m) FFAR type, especially in
warheads and launchers, and notable for its extremely high velocity. Like the
later FZ types of the same calibre, the CRV7 is spin-stabilised by a fluted
exhaust nozzle, has three spring-deployed wrap-round fins at the tail, and is
notable for its combination of good range plus low dispersion, and multiple
warhead options. The latter include unitary, submunition and flechette types
for tasks ranging from anti-ship attack to air-to-air use via anti-tank and close
support missions. The 9.4lb (4.3kg) M151 HE blast fragmentation warhead is
designed for use against vehicles, light armour, soft ground targets,
personnel, light naval craft and helicopters. The 9.7lb (4.4kg) M156 white
phosphorus/incendiary warhead is designed for target-marking. The 17lb
(7.7kg) M229 HE blast fragmentation warhead is designed for use against
vehicles, light armour, soft ground targets, personnel, light naval craft and
helicopters. The 9.4lb (4.3kg) M247 HEDP shaped-charge blast fragmentation
warhead is designed for use against vehicles, light armour, soft ground
targets, personnel, ships and helicopters. The 10.8lb (4.9kg) M257 flare
warhead is designed for night illumination and target marking. The 9.3lb
(4.2kg) WDU-4A/A warhead contains 0.046oz (1.3g) flechettes for use against
vehicles, materiel and personnel in the area-saturation role. The 8.7lb (4.0kg)
WDU-13/A warhead contains 0.137oz (3.9g) flechettes for use against
vehicles, materiel and personnel in the area-saturation role. The 9.4lb (4.3kg)
WTU-1/B and WTU-5001/B warheads are practice types. The 8lb (3.6kg)
WAU-5001/B warhead contains a tungsten rod for use against heavy tanks.
The 8lb (3.6kg) BAH-002 warhead contains a steel rod for use against light
and medium tanks. The 12.4lb (5.6kg) RA-79 warhead is an HE anti-ship type
with a kinetic-energy penetrator combined with a delayed-action blast
fragmentation HE charge for attacks on ships up to 3,000 tons. The 5lb (2.3kg)
BAH-004 warhead is under development with a tungsten penetrator for
long-range use against heavy tanks. The 16lb (7.3kg) WDU-5001/B warhead is
under development with a hardened steel casing and zirconium liner to
penetrate hardened aircraft shelters and cause fires inside them. And the
10lb (4.5kg) WDU-5002/B warhead is under development with six low-drag
tungsten rod flechettes ejected at motor burn-out for use against armour.

THOMSON BRANDT TBA 68

Type: air-to-surface and air-to-air rocket
Dimensions: diameter 0.68m (2.68in); length varies from 0.847 to
1.165m (33.35 to 45.87in) depending on specific warhead type
Weight: total round 4.3 to 6.26kg (9.48 to 13.8lb) depending on specific
warhead type
Warhead: 0.8kg (1.76lb) inert warhead on Type 252 rocket, 1.05kg
(2.31lb) blast warhead on Type 251P rocket, 1.8kg (3.97lb) smoke
warhead on Type 250 rocket, 1.8kg (3.97lb) hollow-charge and
fragmentation warhead on Type 253 rocket, and 3.0kg (6.61lb)
fragmentation on Type 246 rocket
Powerplant: one Type 25 or Type 68F1B solid-propellant rocket
Performance: range 1,000/4,000m (1,095/4,375yd)

The **Thomson Brandt TBA 68** (previously known as the **SNEB 68**) is
amongst the world's most important air-launched rockets, and has been
produced in a number of forms to suit particular purposes. The type can be
carried in a number of fixed- and rotary-wing launcher pods sized between
six and 36 rockets. The layout of the rocket is standard, with a core section
(rocket motor and rail-mounted stabiliser section) to which is added any of
several unitary warhead sections. The rocket is stabilised by eight fins
deployed by propellant gas as the weapon leaves its launch tube, and the
leading edge of each fin is chamfered to impart additional spin-stabilisation.
    If the TBA 68 is the Mk 1 version of this weapon, the **Thomson Brandt
Multi-Dart 260** is the Mk 2 version specifically tailored to the anti-light
armour role with a submunition warhead. The type is fitted with the

Below:
**In addition to the underfuselage fairing that accommodates a 30mm DEFA 553
cannon plus 150 rounds, this Dassault-Breguet/Dornier Alpha Jet E carries four
Matra LR155 launchers for 68mm (2.68in) Thomson Brandt TBA-68 rockets.**
Matra

The value of multiple stores racks is attested by the load carried on the five hardpoints of this SEPECAT Jaguar GR Mk 1: one drop tank on the centreline, four 1,000lb (454kg) bombs on the inner underwing hardpoints, and four Matra launchers for 68mm (2.68in) Thomson Brandt TBA-68 rockets on the outer underwing hardpoints. *BAe*

improved Type 26 or Type 68F solid-propellant rocket motor for ranges between 1,200 and 4,000m (1,315 and 4,375yd). The **Multi-Dart 261-8 ABL** is the baseline model with a 3kg (6.6lb) submunition warhead optimised for use against light armour. The warhead contains eight flechettes each weighing 190g (6.7oz) and capable of piercing 15mm (0.6in) of armour. The Multi-Dart 260 variant optimised for armoured personnel carriers and comparable light materiel is the **Multi-Dart 261-36 AMV**. The warhead of this variant again weighs 3kg (6.6lb) but contains 36 smaller-diameter flechettes each weighing 35g (1.23oz) and capable of piercing 8mm (0.312in) of armour.

This BAe (BAC) Strikemaster Mk 88 of the Royal New Zealand Air Force carries 75Imp gal (341l) drop tanks and Matra launchers for 68mm (2.68in) Thomson Brandt TBA-68 rockets. *BAe*

THOMSON BRANDT TBA 100

Type: air-to-surface rocket
Dimensions: diameter 0.10m (3.94in); length 0.248m (97.64in); fin
 span 0.70m (27.56in)
Weight: total round between 36.9 and 42.6kg (81.3 and 93.9lb)
 depending on specific warhead type
Warhead: 12.5kg (27.6lb) Type LUM illuminating, 14kg (30.9lb) Type
 ESP semi-armour-piercing, 14.4kg (31.7lb) Type ECC hollow-charge
 armour-piercing, 17.6kg (38.8lb) Type EEG general-purpose
 fragmentation, 17.6kg (38.8lb) Type IN inert practice, and 18.2kg
 (40.1lb) Type DEM demolition
Powerplant: one Type 100F1 solid-propellant rocket
Performance: range 1,000/4,000m (1,095/4,375yd)

Though similar to the TBA 68 in basic layout, the **Thomson Brandt
TBA 100** rocket wields a considerably heavier punch at comparable effective
range, though only at the expense of higher weight and, inevitably, smaller
numbers of rockets that can be carried by fixed- and rotary-wing aircraft with
four- and six-round launcher pods. The basic rocket, without its warhead but
including its nose plug and stabilising section, weighs some 24kg (52.9lb),
and the choice of several warhead types adds to the TBA 100's tactical
flexibility.

Like the TBA 68, the TBA 100 has spawned a Mk 2 version in the form of the
Multi-Dart 100, introduced in 1983 for low-level attack against armour. The
Type 100F1 solid-propellant rocket motor is used, and the Multi-Dart 100 is
available with three types of submunition warhead. The Type AB24 warhead
is intended for use against tanks and other heavily armoured targets, and at a
weight of 15.5kg (34.2lb) contains six 1.65kg (3.64lb) flechettes each able to
penetrate 80mm (3.2in) of armour. The Type ABL warhead is designed for
use against armoured personnel carriers and light material, and at a weight
of 14.5kg (32lb) contains 36 190g (6.7oz) flechettes each able to penetrate
15mm (0.6in) of armour. And the Type AMV warhead is designed for use
against light material, and at a weight of 14kg (30.9lb) contains 192 35g
(1.23oz) flechettes able to penetrate 8mm (0.32in) of armour.

Overleaf:
**For its time the Dassault-Breguet Mirage III carried a diverse assortment of
weapons, though it has never been more than an indifferent performer in the
low-level roles. This layout shows off some of the more important types: from
front to back these are the pair of internal 30mm DEFA 552A cannon each with
125 rounds, flanked by two CC420 pods (each containing one 30mm DEFA 553
cannon plus 400 rounds) and two Matra R550 Magic air-to-air missiles;
18 BAP 100 anti-runway bombs with their 14-3-M2 adapter flanked by two
four-tube launchers and their 100mm (3.94in) Thomson Brandt TBA-100
rockets; a drop tank flanked by four combined practice bomb/rocket launcher
pods (with 68mm/2.68in Thomson Brandt TBA-68 rockets and practice bombs)
and two rocket launchers for 68mm (2.68in) rockets; 10 Durandal runway-
cratering bombs, free-fall bombs, two types of Alkan twin tandem adapter
rack with free-fall bombs, and drop tanks.** *MARS*

SNIA BPD MEDUSA

Type: air-to-surface rocket
Dimensions: diameter 0.81m (3.19in); length 1.57m (61.81in) with
    unitary warheads of 1.90m (74.80in) with submunition warhead
Weight: total round 15.9kg (35.1lb) with unitary warheads or 18.9kg
    (41.7lb) with submunition warhead
Warhead: 7kg (15.4lb) HE, pre-formed fragmentation, spotting and
    hollow-charged HE unitary types, or 10kg (22.0lb) submunition type
Powerplant: one SNIA-Viscosa solid-propellant rocket
Performance: burn-out velocity 650m (2,133ft)/sec with unitary
    warheads or 550m (1,804ft)/sec with submunition warhead; range
    1,400 to 6,000m (1,530 to 6,560yd)

The **SNIA BPD Medusa** is a powerful medium-calibre air-to-surface rocket
designed for use in six-, seven- and 12-round launcher pods carried by fixed-
and rotary-wing aircraft. The Medusa is stabilised by a combination of spin
(imparted by thrust deflectors in the rocket motor's exhaust nozzle) and triple
wrap-round fins at the tail. A warhead containing 11 anti-tank and
anti-personnel submunitions is under development for this important rocket
system.

Below:
**Featuring a highly appropriate civil registration, the prototype of the
Aermacchi MB339K Veltro 2 light attack aircraft shows off a portion of its
weapon-carriage capability in addition to its inbuilt pair of 30mm DEFA 554
cannon each with 125 rounds; the inner hardpoints carry bombs, and the outer
hardpoints each support an Aerea launcher for 81mm (3.2in) SNIA-BPD
Medusa rockets.** *IMPPS*

SNIA BPD FALCO

Type: air-to-surface rocket
Dimensions: diameter 0.122m (4.8in); length (122/A) 2.535m (99.8in)
with unitary warheads or 3.041m (119.72in) with submunition
warheads, and (122/H) 2.716m (106.93in) with unitary warheads or
3.344m (131.65in) with submunition warheads
Weight: total round (122/A) 59.9kg (132.1lb) with unitary warheads or
65.9kg (145.3lb) with submunition warheads, and (122/H) 58.4kg
(128.7lb) with unitary warheads or 71.4kg (157.4lb) with submunition
warheads
Warhead: (122/A) 26kg (57.3lb) unitary types (HE and hollow-charge
HE), or 32kg (70.5lb) submunition types (APM with 66 anti-personnel
mines, or ATM with seven anti-tank mines, or APAMB with 77
anti-personnel and anti-materiel bomblets), and (122/H) 19kg
(41.9lb) unitary types (HE, white phosphorus, smoke and target
practice), or 32kg (70.5lb) submunition types (APM with 66
anti-personnel mines, or ATM with seven anti-tank mines or APAMB
with 77 anti-personnel and anti-materiel bomblets)
Powerplant: one SNIA-Viscosa solid-propellant rocket (short type for
aircraft-launched 122/A and long type for helicopter-launched 122/H)
Performance: burn-out velocity 750m (2,461ft)/sec with unitary
warhead or 670m (2,198ft)/sec with submunition warhead

The **SNIA BPD Falco** is a series of very powerful air-to-surface rockets
developed from the same company's FIROS field artillery rocket system and
notable for its range and wide assortment of warhead types. The **Falco
122/A** aircraft-launched version uses a shorter motor, and is optimised for
stand-off attacks against area targets or shorter range attacks on point
targets of the armoured and unarmoured types. The type is fired from a
four-round launcher pod. The **Falco 122/H** is the helicopter-launched variant
of the family using a longer motor to offset the lower launch speed imposed
by helicopter operations. Helicopters can carry three- or six-round launcher
pods.

BOFORS M70

Type: air-to-surface rocket
Dimensions: diameter 0.135m (5.315in); length 2.105m (82.87in) with general-purpose warhead or 2.165m (85.24in) with armour-piercing warhead
Weight: total round 45.8kg (101.0lb) with general-purpose warhead or 44.6kg (98.3lb) with armour-piercing warhead
Warhead: 19.6kg (43.2lb) hollow-charge armour-piercing, 20.8kg (45.9lb) general-purpose, and 20.8kg (45.9lb) inert practice
Powerplant: one Bofors solid-propellant rocket
Performance: burn-out velocity 600m (1,969ft)/sec; range 2,000m (2,185yd)

The **Bofors M70** rocket was designed as part of the weapon fit for the Saab 37 Viggen multi-role aircraft, and is an extremely powerful weapon which can carry either of two operational warheads. The rockets can be fired singly or in a ripple at 0.1sec intervals. The anti-tank warhead contains a 5kg (11lb) charge, and the general-purpose warhead contains a 3.7kg (8.2lb) charge. The rocket is fired from a six-round launcher pod.

OERLIKON-BÜHRLE/SNIA BPD SNORA

Type: air-to-surface rocket
Dimensions: diameter 0.81m (3.19in); length varies from 1.416 to 1.785m (55.75 to 70.28in) depending on specific warhead type
Weight: 13.2 to 19.7kg (29.1 to 43.4lb) depending on specific warhead type
Warhead: 4kg (8.8lb) target practice, 4.5kg (9.9lb) hollow-charge anti-tank and HE pre-formed fragmentation, 5kg (11.0lb) target practice, 7kg (15.4lb) target practice and HE pre-formed fragmentation, and 11kg (24.3lb) target practice and HE pre-formed fragmentation
Powerplant: one Oerlikon-Bührle TWK 006 solid-propellant rocket
Performance: range about 2,500m (2,735yd)

Developed jointly in Switzerland and Italy as the **Oerlikon-Bührle/SNIA BPD SNORA** series, this is amongst the most widley used weapons of its type in the world. The basic rocket is powered by the TWK 006 motor section, which weighs 8.7kg (19.2lb) and comes complete with the wrap-round fins that help to stabilise this spinning rocket. To this core is added the warhead/fuse section to make up the individual type. The rockets are designed for use by fixed-wing aircraft (in four-, six- and 12-round launcher pods) and helicopters (in seven-round launcher pods).

OERLIKON-BÜHRLE SURA-D

Type: air-to-surface rocket
Dimensions: diameter 0.81m (3.19in); length 1.077 to 1.212m (42.4 to 47.72in) depending on specific warhead type
Weight: 12.7 to 14.2kg (28.0 to 31.3lb) depending on specific warhead type
Warhead: 3kg (6.6lb) target practice, 3kg (6.6lb) HE pre-formed fragmentation, 3kg (6.6lb) HE incendiary, 3kg (6.6lb) hollow-charge anti-tank, 4.5kg (9.9lb) target practice and 4.5kg (9.9lb) HE pre-formed fragmentation
Powerplant: one Oerlikon-Bührle TWK 007 solid-propellant rocket
Performance: burn-out velocity varies from 530 to 595m (1,739 to 1,952ft)/sec depending on variant; range 2,500m (2,735yd)

The **Oerlikon-Bührle SURA-D** is an upgraded version of the out-of-service SURA-FL designed for use by a wide variety of fixed- and rotary-wing aircraft used against point or area targets. The rocket is based on the TWK 007 motor section, whose exhaust deflectors provide the rocket with spin stabilisation. The motor section weighs 8.4kg (18.5lb) and can accommodate any of seven warhead types. A particular advantage of the SURA-D rocket is that it needs no special launcher pod. Before launch the cruciform fin assembly serves as the forward suspension (being attached to the front suspension lug on any NATO-standard hardpoint), and below this uppermost rocket can be attached in similar manner a tier of more SURA-D rockets. The rockets are launched electrically from the bottom weapon upwards, the sliding fin assembly serving as a guide until the rear cone connects with it, whereupon the fin assembly is detached from the tier to serve as the rocket's tail-mounted stabilising unit.

Right:
The 81mm (3.2in) Oerlikon-Bührle SURA is admirably configured for use on light helicopters such as the Bell 204/205 series. *Oerlikon-Bührle*

BEI DEFENSE SYSTEMS HYDRA 70

Type: air-to-air and air-to-surface rocket
Dimensions: diameter 2.75in (0.6985m); length 46.85in (1.19m); fin span 10.0in (0.254m)
Weight: varies between 18.96 and 26.23lb (8.6 and 11.9kg) depending on specific warhead type
Warhead: see below
Powerplant: one solid-propellant rocket
Performance: range 550/9,650yd (505/8,825m)

The **Mk 4 2.75in FFAR** (Folding-Fin Aircraft Rocket) is a classic and very widely used tactical weapon with 6.5in (0.165m) folding tail fins. The FFAR was developed in the USA as the 'Mighty Mouse' series in the air-to-air role with a 6lb (2.7kg) warhead, developing in the 1960s to a 10lb (4.5kg) warhead and ultimately to a 17lb (7.7kg) type with a rocket motor providing sufficient thrust for a range of between 550 and 6,500yd (505 and 5,945m), 3,750yd (3,430m) being the maximum effective range. However, the velocity of the rocket is insufficient to free the weapon from the worst effects of gravity drop and crosswind. The Mk 4 is designed for use with high-performance fixed-wing aircraft.

The **Mk 40 2.75in FFAR** is the Mk 4 variant optimised for use by helicopters. It has a scarfed nozzle for greater spin (and thus greater accuracy) when launched from low-speed platforms. Warheads associated with the Mk 4 and Mk 40 versions of the original FFAR are the 10lb (4.5kg) M151 HE, white phosphorus or anti-personnel fragmentation, 10lb M156 chemical, 17lb (7.7kg) M229 HE white phosphorus or anti-personnel fragmentation, and Northrop WDU-4A/A submunition warhead with about 3,000 flechettes.

The **BEI Defense Systems Mk 66 2.75in Hydra 70** is the most important of current weapons, produced in the USA as part of the Hydra 70 system. This model has a higher-impulse rocket motor developed for the US Navy, giving a burn-out velocity in the order of 3,280ft (1,000m)/sec. This generates greater range in both the air-to-air and air-to-surface roles, and also provides better accuracy in combination with the revised arrangement of four wrap-round fins. The Mk 66 can be used by fixed- and rotary-wing aircraft, and can carry a useful assortment of warhead types: the M151, M247 hollow-charge anti-tank; M255 submunition type with about 2,500 tiny flechettes for use against battlefield targets ranging from other helicopters to exposed personnel; M261 multi-purpose submunition type with capabilities against armour, material and personnel as a result of its nine M73 hollow-charge fragmentation submunitions; M262 illuminating type; M264 smokescreen type; and an as-yet unstandardised chaff type. The 2.75in FFAR and Hydra 70 rockets can be fired from fixed- and rotary-wing aircraft using a number of different launcher pods.

7: Cluster Bombs & Dispensers

FRANCE

MATRA DURANDAL

Type: medium anti-runway bomb
Dimensions: diameter 0.223m (8.78in); length 2.70m (106.3in), fin span 0.43m (16.93in)
Weight: total round 219kg (482.8lb)
Warhead: 100kg (220.5lb) including 15kg (33.1lb) of explosive

The **Matra Durandal** is an important runway-cratering weapon, and began to enter service in 1977. The weapon is carried on standard suspension lugs and needs no special control equipment. On release at any height down to 60m (195ft) at speeds between 650 and 1,020km/hr (404 and 634mph), the Durandal is retarded by a double parachute and its nose begins to drop.

Below:
The Matra Durandal is a simple yet highly effective runway-cratering munition, using a parachute retarder to get the weapon clear of the low-level launch aircraft, and then a solid propellant booster rocket to drive it through the runway after the parachute has pitched down the munition's nose. These Durandals are carried by a Dassault-Breguet Mirage F1 in company with Matra R550 Magic air-to-air missiles. *Matra*

When the optimum no-ricochet penetration angle ($-20°$ to $-30°$) has been reached, the retarder is released and the bomb's rocket motor is ignited. The weapon is then accelerated to impact the runway at a velocity of some 260m (853ft)/sec, sufficient for the forged steel warhead to pierce 400mm (15.75in) of concrete. The fuse system has a 1sec delay, and detonates the warhead under the runway's surface to create a crater 2m (6.56ft) deep and 2.5m (8.2ft) in radius, plus heave damage to a radius of 3.5m (11.5ft); the damage area is increased to 250sq m (300sq yd) by fractures. The weapon is designed for use in multiple launches for maximum effect, double diagonal attacks (each delivery six, nine or 10 Durandals) being considered the best way of rendering a standard runway inoperative for one day. The Durandal is used by the US Air Force with the designation **CBU-15**, and by another 10 export customers.

FRANCE

MATRA/THOMSON BRANDT BLG 66 BELOUGA

Type: medium cluster bomb
Dimensions: diameter 0.36m (14.17in); length 3.30m (129.92in); fin
   span 0.58m (22.83in)
Weight: total round 290kg (639.33lb)
Warhead: 181.2kg (399.5lb) comprising 152 1.2kg (2.65lb) bomblets

---

The **Matra/Thomson Brandt BLG 66 Belouga** is the standard French cluster bomb. The type was developed in the 1970s as successor to the Giboulée cluster bomb, the objectives being lower drag, a larger ground pattern for the dispensed bomblets, and the ability to be launched at higher speeds (anything up to 1,020km/h [634mph]). The weapon is delivered as a certified round of ammunition, and the cylindrical mid-section of the weapon is filled with 19 rows of eight rearward-facing ejector tubes for 0.66mm (2.6in) bomblets.

   These 152 bomblets are of three types: general-purpose fragmentation (for use against motor transport, parked aircraft and dumps) anti-tank and area interdiction. Before releasing the weapon the pilot chooses between two operating patterns, namely a length of 120 or 240m (395 or 785ft) by a width of 40 or 60m (130 or 195ft). On release down to a minimum height of 60m (195ft), the sequencer in the weapon's nose deploys a drag chute to allow the aircraft to clear the area before bomblet release at regular intervals to each side of the dispenser. The bomblets are themselves retarded, and reach the ground vertically; the general-purpose bomblet detonates into a disc of horizontal fragments, and the HEAT bomblet type explodes downwards on hitting the top of an armoured vehicle, the penetration capability being 250mm (9.8in).

Below:
Light and possessing a low drag factor, the Belouga bomblet dispenser can be carried in multiples by light aircraft such as this Dassault-Breguet/Dornier Alpha Jet E. This load of four Belougas would saturate a substantial area with 604 bomblets. *Matra*

THOMSON BRANDT BAP 100

Type: light anti-runway bomb
Dimensions: diameter 0.10m (3.94in); length 1.78m (70.08in)
Weight: total round 32.5kg (71.6lb)
Warhead: 18kg (39.7lb) including 3.6kg (7.9lb) of explosive

Development of the **Thomson Brandt BAP 100** (Bombe Anti-Piste 100mm, or 100mm anti-runway bomb) began in the mid-1970s to provide the French Air Force with a lightweight counterpart to the heavier Durandal. The weapon (carried in multiples of nine) is released as the launch aircraft approaches the target runway on a diagonal course, the launch height being between 50 and 80m (165 and 260ft), and the launch speed between 630 and 1,040km/hr (391 and 646mph). The weapon's onboard sequencer is activated after 0.5sec and opens the tail to deploy a braking parachute with the bomb 3m (10ft) below the aircraft. Thereafter the warhead is armed, the motor ignition sequence started, the parachute released and the motor fired to boost the bomb obliquely downard at 65° through the runway at between 230 and 260m (755 and 853ft)/sec. The warhead can penetrate 1,000mm (39.4in) of reinforced concrete, and can destroy 50sq m (60sq yd) of concrete 300mm (11.8in) thick when detonated at any delay up to 6hr.

THOMSON BRANDT BAT 120

Type: light anti-armour bomb
Dimensions: diameter 0.12m (4.72in); length 1.50m (59.06in)
Weight: total round 34kg (75.0lb)
Warhead: 24kg (52.9lb) blast fragmentation including 6kg (13.2lb) of explosive

Partner to the BAP 100 and carried in the same multiples of nine, the **Thomson Brandt BAT 120** (Bombe d'Appui Tactique 120mm, or 120mm tactical attack bomb) has a retarding parachute in the tail but no booster rocket. The warhead is based on that of a Thomson Brandt 120mm (4.72in) mortar bomb, and has sections in front of and behind the central suspension/ejector unit. After release at low altitude and any speed between 650 and 1,020km/hr (404 and 634mph), the bomb is retarded by the parachute and falls at 80° to reach the ground at a speed of 20m (65ft)/sec. The weapon is detonated just above the ground by a piezo-electric fuse, and the focused burst of the front and rear charges produces two nearly horizontal discs of fragments moving at 1,200m (3,937ft)/sec to a radius of 30m (100ft). The BAT

120 comes in two subvariants, namely the **BAT 120 ABL** for use against light armour, and the **BAT 120 AMV** for use against unarmoured targets. The former sprays 800 12.5g (0.44oz) main and many smaller fragments capable of penetrating 7mm (0.28in) of steel over a radius of 20m (66ft), and the latter scatters 2,600 4g (0.14oz) fragments capable of penetrating 4mm (0.16in) of steel over the same radius.

FRANCE

THOMSON BRANDT BM 400

Type: heavy modular bomb
Dimensions: diameter 0.32m (12.6in); length 3.30m (129.92in)
Weight: total round 390kg (859.8lb)
Warhead: three 100kg (220.5lb) parachute-retarded modules

The **Thomson Brandt BM 400** modular (cluster) bomb was designed in the late 1970s and early 1980s for the destruction of high-value hard and area targets after release at any speed between 650 and 1,100km/hr (404 and 684mph) at a height of 30m (100ft). The notion behind the weapon is greater efficiency than a single 'slick' or retarded bomb combined with lower cost than a standard cluster bomb. The weapon can be released horizontally, or in a loft manoeuvre for a stand-off range of 5,000m (5,470yd) or 10,000m (10,935yd) when the weapon is fitted with an optional rocket booster. The BM 400 consists of a cylindrical 90kg (198.4lb) fin-stabilised sleeve containing three explosive modules (two modules in the smaller **BM 250**). As the weapon is released, a windmill-powered sequencer starts the parachute-extraction of the modules from the rear of the casing at preset intervals. Each module has one of two types of pre-fragmented warhead, and drops vertically to detonate at a height of 0.7m (27.6in) as the nose probe touches the ground. Of the two warhead types, one is designed to deal with harder targets (concentrations of light armour, ammunition dumps and radar installations) and bursts into some 700 or 800 80g (2.82oz) fragments that fly out in a flat disc at a velocity of 2,000m (6,652ft)/sec; these can pierce 17mm (0.67in) of armour at a radius of 50m (165ft), or 12mm (0.47in) of armour at 100m (330ft). The other warhead type is designed for softer targets (transport and troop concentrations) and bursts into 1,500 larger and many smaller fragments; the larger fragments can pierce 12mm (0.47in) of steel at a radius of 50m (165ft) or 7mm (0.28in) at 100m (330ft). A spacing of 200m (220yd) between the modules allows a single BM 400 to saturate an area 600m (655yd) long by 100m (110yd) wide with a devastating hail of heavy fragments. Thomson Brandt is developing two important new submunitions for the BM 400: the SMABL is derived from the warhead of the BAT 120 bomb, and at a weight of 20kg (44.1lb) and length of 670mm (26.38in) shatters into 500 fragments; and the SMAP is derived from the warhead of the BAP 100, and at a weight of 23kg (50.7lb) and length of 1,000m (39.37in) has the same performance as the BAP 100.

MBB MW-1

Type: submunition dispenser
Dimensions: width 0.150m (59.06in); height 0.7m (27.56in); length
   5.30m (208.66in)
Weight: total dispenser about 5,000kg (11,023lb)
Warhead: about 4,000kg (8,818lb) of submunitions

The **MBB MW-1** (Mehrzweckwaffe Nr 1, or multiple dispenser weapon No 1)
was developed for the Panavia Tornado multi-role aircraft of the West
German Air Force, and began to enter service in 1984. The MW-1 is a large
dispenser that fits on to the Tornado's underfuselage suspension lugs. The
complete dispenser is made up of four 28-tube sub-units (two rectilinear
sections and two modestly streamlined nose and tail sections) for a total of
112 0.132m (5.2in) diameter double-ended launcher tubes. The submunitions
can be loaded with different ejection charges to provide different lateral
ranges to produce the intended patterns, which are designed primarily for
employment against armour and airfield depending on the mix of
submunitions. These come in six varieties: the ASW for attacks on hardened
aircraft shelters, the KB44 for attacks on armour, the MIFF minelet again for
anti-tank use, the MUSA minelet for attacks on personnel and soft-skinned
vehicles, the MUSPA airfield-denial minelet, and the STABO for cratering
runways. With all its submunitions dispensed, the empty MW-1 is designed
to be jettisoned (despite the fact that it constitutes some 10% of the cost of
each system) because of its high drag.

Below:
**This underview of a Panavia Tornado in West German service highlights the
sheer bulk of the four-part MW-1 dispenser. In combat the dispenser would be
jettisoned once emptied to reduce drag and so facilitate the Tornado's egress
from the scene of action.** *Panavia*

Above:
Seen with an IAI Kfir-C1 is the weapons layout generally used with the upgraded Kfir-C2 fitted with canard foreplanes and dogtoothed outer wing panels (amongst other features) for enhanced manoeuvrability and controllability. Amongst this selection of gun, bomb, rocket and missile armament are TAL cluster bombs (outer ends of the free-fall ordnance 'vee').
Israel Aircraft Industries

RAFAEL ARMAMENT AUTHORITY TAL-1 AND TAL-2

> *Type:* light cluster bomb
> *Dimensions:* diameter 0.406m (16.0in); length 2.345m (92.32in); fin span 0.56m (22.05in)
> *Weight:* total round 250kg (551.1lb) for TAL-1 and 236kg (520.3lb) for TAL-2
> *Warhead:* 139.5kg (307.5lb) and 126kg (277.8lb) of bomblets for TAL-1 and TAL-2 respectively

Introduced in 1981, the **Rafael TAL-1** is a simple but useful cluster bomb containing 279 0.5g (17.64oz) bomblets. Each of the latter contains 0.16kg (5.64oz) of HE, which breaks the casing into 1,800 anti-personnel and anti-vehicle fragments effective to a radius of 8m (26ft). Before the casing is opened it is spun by its fins as an aid to bomblet dispersal. The fuse system allows the casing to open only when the bomb is well clear of the launch aircraft. The coverage of a single bomb can be as great as 53,000sq m (63,390sq yd). The **TAL-2** is an improved variant introduced in 1983, and differes from its predecessor in having 315 0.4kg (14.1oz) bomblets (but with the same explosive charge and number of fragments as the slightly larger bomblets of the TAL-1) and aerodynamic rather than mechanical fusing.

SPAIN

EXPLOSIVOS ALAVESES BRFA-330

> *Type:* medium runway-cratering bomb
> *Dimensions:* diameter 0.3m (11.81in); length 3.044m (119.84in); fin span 0.6m (23.62in)
> *Weight:* total round 330kg (727.5lb)
> *Warhead:* 75kg (165.3lb) of HE

The **Explosivos Alaveses BRFA-330** is a powerful runway-attack weapon for use by high-performance aircraft fitted with NATO standard suspension lugs, though the weapon can also be supplied to order with Warsaw Pact standard attachment capability. The weapon is designed for low-altitude attack with a minimum release height of 80m (265ft) at any speed between 520 and 1,110km/hr (323 and 690mph). Immediately after it has been released the weapon deploys its braking parachute, allowing the launch aircraft to clear the area and pitching down the bomb's nose. The parachute is then released and a rocket motor in the tail ignited to accelerate the weapon through the runway and into the earth to a depth of 0.6m (23.6in), where the warhead is detonated to cause crater, fracture and heave damage over an area of some 200 to 250sq m (240 to 300sq yd).

FFV M71 VIRGO

Type: light fragmentation bomb
Dimensions: diameter 0.214m (8.425in); length 1.90m (74.8in) with
    nose fuse and parachute retarder pack; fin span 0.368m (14.49in)
Weight: total round 123kg (271.2lb)
Warhead: 30kg (66.1lb) of RDX/TNT inside a casing of steel fragments

Though small and comparatively light, the **FFV M71 Virgo** is a powerful and
apparently effective fragmentation weapon with capability against all types
of targets likely to be tackled by the Swedish Air Force during an invasion of
Sweden. The Virgo has a single-point attachment (including a safety device)
to the launch aircraft, and possesses three main sections connected by the
weapon's central tube. The forward end is the proximity fuse that detonates
the weapon a few metres above the ground or any thick vegetation. In the
centre is the warhead with an explosive filling inside a pre-fragmented
casing, and at the rear is the plastic tail section accommodating the
parachute retarter.

SWITZERLAND

SPICE CH-TABO

Type: medium bomblet dispenser
Dimensions: not revealed
Weight: not revealed
Warhead: typically seven bomblets

The **SPICE CH-TABO** is a development by the Swiss companies F+W
(Federal Aircraft Factory, which has design and marketing leadership) and
the Federal Ammunition Factory at Thun, with marketing undertaken by
Matra. The dispenser is a pylon-mounted container which typically holds
seven special bomblets optimised for attacks on soft (personnel, motor
transport etc) and semi-hard (material etc) targets. Each bomblet is a
spherical casing over an explosive core and 8,000 cast steel balls. Ejected
from the container by air pressure, each bomblet falls towards the ground,
stabilised and retarded by a cast aluminium tail fan, which spins the bomblet
as an aid to warhead dispersion. The bomblet is fitted with either a
mechanical fuse (using a telescopic stand-off probe) or an electronic
proximity fuse for air-burst at a height of some 70 to 100cm (26.6 to 39.4in)
above the ground. Using the latter type of fusing, two CH-TABO containers
can saturate an area 50m (165ft) in width and 200m (655ft) in length with four
fragments per 1sq m (10.75sq ft) after bomblet release at low altitude.

HUNTING ENGINEERING HADES

Type: medium cluster bomb
Dimensions: diameter 16.5in (0.419m); length 96.5in (2.451m); fin
span 22.25in (0.565m)
Weight: total round 582lb (264.0kg)
Warhead: 49 HB876 area-denial minelets

The **Hunting Engineering HADES** (Hunting Area DEnial System) cluster
bomb combines the dispenser of the BL755 dispenser bomb with the HB876
area-denial minelet of the JP233 anti-airfield dispenser system. The weapon
works in exactly the same way as the BL755, but the payload comprises 49
5.5lb (2.5kg) HB876 minelets. These free-fall to the ground after being
dispensed in the air, right themselves on their radial rings of sprung legs, and
await detonation by any close-by disturbance. The individual minelets
self-destruct after a variable but preset interval if not previously detonated.

Below:
**The Hunting Engineering HADES is essentially the casing of the BL755 filled
with the HB876 area-denial minelets of the JP233 dispenser weapon.**
Hunting Engineering Ltd 20598/M

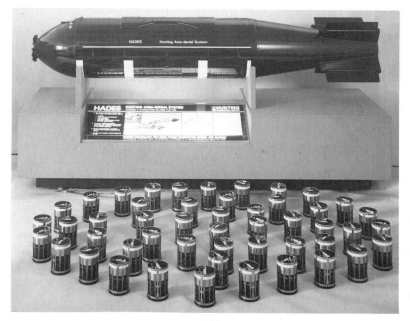

HUNTING ENGINEERING BL755

> *Type:* medium cluster bomb
> *Dimensions:* diameter 16.5in (0.419m); length 96.5in (2.451m); fin
>   span 22.25in (0.565m)
> *Weight:* total round 582lb (264.0kg)
> *Warhead:* 147 anti-tank/fragmentation bomblets

The **Hunting Engineering BL755** is a dual-role weapon that entered service
in 1972, and is designed to provide a high 'kill' probability against a range of
hard and soft targets. Before the aircraft takes off one of four time delays is
set on the weapon to ensure adequate separation of the aircraft and weapon

Above:
**This McDonnell Douglas Phantom FGR Mk 2 multi-role combat aircraft carries
a heavy mixed armament: four AIM-7E Sparrow and four AIM-9B Sidewinder
air-to-air missiles, and no fewer than six Hunting Engineering BL755 cluster
bombs.** *MoD (RAF)*

before the latter is fully activated. When the bomb is dropped the primary striker is armed and, after the set interval, fires the initial cartridge which produces the gas pressure to blow off the two-part body skins and then fires the main cartridge. This latter ejects the bomblets, which are accommodated seven to each of the weapon's 21 bays. Each 2.68in (0.068m) diameter bomblet is 5.91in (0.15m) long as it is fired, lengthening to 14.0in (0.356m) as the spring tail and nose probe deploy. The bomblet is armed as it falls, and detonates on impact with the shaped-charge warhead able to penetrate at least 250mm (9.84in) of armour as well as scattering a cloud of at least 2,000 lethal fragments.

Entering service in 1987, the **Improved BL755** is a much developed version of the original BL755 but carrying considerably more powerful bomblets using the latest shaped-charge techniques. Each bomblet is still of the same 2.68in (0.068m) diameter, but is 5.87in (0.149m) long as it is fired, extending to 24.69in (0.627m) complete with extending nose probe and retarding parachute.

UK

HUNTING ENGINEERING JP233

Type: heavy airfield-attack and area-denial submunition dispenser
Dimensions: width 33.07in (0.84m); height 23.6in (0.599m) for underfuselage configuration and for underwing configuration with SG357 submunitions, or 22.0in (0.556m) for underwing configuration with HB876 submunitions; length 257.9in (6.551m) for underfuselage configuration, 223.5in (5.677m) for underwing configuration with SG357 submunitions, and 166.9in (4.24m) for underwing configuration with HB876 submunitions; fin span 63.07in (1.602m) for underwing configuration with SG357 submunitions, and 53.39in (1.356m) for underwing configuration with HB876 submunitions
Weight: total system 5,148lb (2,335.1kg) for underfuselage configuration, 3,020lb (1,369.9kg) for underwing configuration with SG357 submunitions, and 2.535lb (1,149.9kg) for underwing configuration with HB876 submunitions
Warhead: (underfuselage twin configuration) 30 SG357 concrete-penetrating and 215 HB876 area-denial submunitions

Used only by the Royal Air Force, though qualified for use on the tactical aircraft of several other nations, the **Hunting Engineering JP233** is a dispenser system designed for decisive blows against major target areas. The system is available in different sizes to suit particular aircraft, the most impressive being that on the Panavia Tornado: two side-by-side containers under the fuselage. These each contain 30 runway-cratering and 215 area-denial submunitions, the dispensing of the two types simultaneously destroying the target and making it difficult for the enemy to move back into the area and effect repairs. The 57lb (25.85kg) SG357 is a substantial submunition comparable to the STABO used in the West German MW-1 dispenser system. Under its retarder it falls nearly vertically to the ground, where the impact fuse fires the hollow-charge primary warhead to open a hole through which the second charge is fired, penetrating into the earth before it detonates to make a crater and a large area of fracture and heave damage. The HB876 area-denial minelet effectively slows enemy repair teams, for these 5.5lb (2.5kg) free-fall minelets are fitted with a disturbance fuse and a variable but preset self-destruct fuse. Its warhead is designed to produce both a high-velocity slug capable of destroying vehicles and a hail of highly destructive steel fragments.

Above:
Partnering the SG357 in the JP233 system, and also used in the BL755 and some US weapons, the HB876 is a capable area-denial minelet. In the JP233 system it is designed to prevent or hinder the work of crews seeking to repair the damage caused by the SG357 submunitions. *Avco Systems Division*

AMERICAN SUBMUNITIONS AND CLUSTER UNITS

The American BLU (Bomb Live Unit) designation covers a considerable number of weapons and weapon types, ranging from small submunitions carried by CBU (Cluster Bomb Unit) and SUU (Suspended Underwing Unit) series dispensers to large special ordnance items. The series was originated in the 1960s to supersede earlier anti-personnel and anti-armour fragmentation weapons, based on the notion that BLUs could be developed comparatively easily for packaging in various numbers into SUUs, which thus became specific CBUs. The two more important SUU varieties are the dropped types, designed to hinge open in the air and release a mass of BLUs which are dispersed by their own aerodynamic surfaces, and the fixed type (of which the SUU-7 was the first), designed to remain under the wing of the launch aircraft and use compressed air to dispense rearwards one or more streams of BLUs, being jettisoned only after the BLUs have been dispensed. The BLUs and CBUs are too numerous for full exposition here, and thus only the most important and modern are mentioned.

The **BLU-73/B** is a fuel/air explosive canister fitted with a retarding drogue. The weapon weighs 100lb (45kg) and contains 72lb (33kg) of ethylene oxide. Three such weapons in an SUU-49 dispenser make up the 500lb (227kg) **CBU-55/B** cluster bomb. Three BLU-73/B bombs are also carried in the **CBU-72** cluster bomb: once dropped, the dispenser is split to free the BLU-73s for their retarded fall; at a height of 30ft (9m) a proximity fuse detonates the charge in each BLU-73 to create an aerosol cloud of fuel and air 60ft (18.3m) in diameter and 8ft (2.4m) thick, which falls to the surface. It is then ignited by another detonator to create an expanding wave front whose 300lb/sq in (22kg/sq cm) overpressure flattens everything within a circle of 60ft (18.3m) radius and causes great damage beyond this radius. The BLU-73/B core is also employed in the US Army's **FAESHED** (Fuel/Air Explosive HElicopter Delivered) weapon, which is the US Navy's **CBU-55** revised for helicopter delivery. The FAE weapon has also proved successful in minefield clearance by detonating all presure-fused mines within a 29ft (8.8m) and all trip-fused mines within an 85ft (25.9m) radius. A similar weapon used by the US Marine Corps is the **MADFAE** (Mass Air Delivery Fuel/Air Explosive). This consists of fin-stabilised aluminium racks, each holding 12 136lb (62kg) FAE units, carried on the external hook of large helicopters for individual or salvo release over minefields.

The **BLU-76/B 'Pave Pat II'** is a fuel-air explosive weapon designed primarily for high-speed delivery but possessing the same low-speed capability as the BLU-72/B. The BLU-76/B contains a higher ethylene oxide payload, but requires four seconds for the formation of the aerosol cloud before the second detonation can be started.

The **PLU-77/B** (sic) is an anti-tank fragmentation bomblet with the capability of discriminating between hard and soft targets, and has a secondary anti-personnel function. A load of 717 such bomblets in a Mk 7 Mod 3 dispenser constitute the US Air Force's 750lb (340kg) **CBU-59/B** cluster bomb, otherwise known as the '**Rockeye II**'.

The **BLU-82/B** is a 15,000lb (6,804kg) general-purpose bomb used mainly for the clearing of helicopter landing zones in jungle. In the **BLU-82/B Mod 'Big Blue 82'** version the warhead comprises 12,600lb (5,715kg) of gelled slurry blast explosive detonated just above the ground level to create a 1,000lb/sq in (73.3kg/sq cm) overpressure.

The **BLU-86A/B** is a steel-cased fragmentation bomblet. A load of 670 such bomblets in a SUU-30A/B dispenser constitutes the 815lb (370kg) **CBU-71** cluster bomb, while 1,800 of the bomblets can be used as an alternative load for the BLU-63/Bs in the **CBU-75A/B** cluster bomb.

The **BLU-95/B** is a 500lb (227kg) fuel/air explosive weapon containing 300lb (136kg) of propylene oxide. Development of this weapon was undertaken for the US Air Force with the initial designation **HSF-1** (High-Speed FAE No 1).

The **BLU-96/B** is a 2,000lb (907kg) fuel/air explosive weapon containing 1,400lb (635kg) of propylene oxide. The BLU-96 is a payload carried by the GBU-15 guided glide bomb, and development was undertaken for the US Air Force with the initial designation **HSF-11**.

The **BLU-108/B** is a US Air Force submunition carrying four Avco Skeet devices. The Skeet is the world's first production 'self-forging fragment' weapon, wobbling through the air so that its onboard infra-red sensor can detect a tank, the guidance system then taking the Skeet directly over the target to detonate an explosive sheet that imparts very high downward velocity to a slab of heavy alloy, at the same time turning it into a streamlined self-forging fragment that hits the tank's weakest armour with a speed of 9,000ft (2,743m)/sec. The BLU-108/B is used as the payload of the CBU-97/B Sensor-Fused Weapon.

The **BLU-109/B** is the **Improved 2,000lb Warhead**, designed to provide US Air Force tactical aircraft with a capability against major hardened targets in succession to the Mk 84 general-purpose bomb, designed in the 1950s and using a low-grade steel case of very limited penetration capability. The BLU 109/B has a high grade steel casing 1in (25.4mm) thick. The warhead is 14.5in (0.368m) in diameter and 95in (2.413m) in length, and is compatible with a number of guidance packages for increased accuracy. Typical are the GBU-10 'Paveway II' laser system, the GBU-15 electro-optical or infra-red systems (including the extended-range capability of the AGM-130 rocket-boosted version), and the GBU-24 'Paveway III' low-level laser system.

The **CBU-87/B** was designed to replace the 'Rockeye' series and other elderly types such as the CBU-58, as this 950lb (431kg) weapon is otherwise known as the **Combined Effects Munition** to tackle all types of target (armour, materiel and personnel) with a single dispensed payload of bomblets. The CBU-87/B is based on the SUU-65/B dispenser and BLU-97/B submunition, and is designed for delivery at any height over 200ft (60m) and at any speed up to 805mph (1,295km/hr). Each bomblet has a pre-fragmented anti-personnel case over a hollow-charge anti-tank warhead, and a disc of incendiary zirconium is also built into the charge to add to the weapon's destructive capability. The fragmentation section can disable motor transport at a range of 50ft (15m) and aircraft at 250ft (76m).

The **CBU-89/B** is one of the US services' most important cluster munitions, an air-delivered scatterable mine system for which the US Air Force is the lead service with the US Army responsible for the **BLU-91/B** and **BLU-92/B** submunitions, and the US Navy for the mine-dispenser adapter. The 700lb (318kg) weapon comprises the SUU-64/B Tactical Munitions Dispenser containing 72 BLU-91/B Gator anti-tank bomblets and 22 BLU-92/B

Gator anti-personnel bomblets. The weapon can be dropped at any altitude between 200 and 40,000ft (60 and 12,190m), the bomblets being dispensed on command of a time fuse or an optional proximity fuse.

The **CBU-92/B** is the **Extended-Range Anti-armor Munition** currently under development for service entry with US Air Force tactical aircraft during 1993 as part of the Wide-Area Anti-armor Munitions programme. The 950lb (431kg) weapon is based on the SUU-65/B dispenser filled with nine anti-tank and three unspecified area-denial submunitions, which are dispensed on command of a time fuse or optional proximity fuse. The ERAM submunition falls under its individual parachute retarder, and on the ground is stabilised by four legs before three-probe seismic/acoustic fuse system is activated. The fuse classifies any target within a range of 500ft (152m), fixes its range and bearing from the submunition, and fires one of the submunition's two Avco Skeet warheads in the right direction. The Skeet's own infra-red fusing system then detonates the warhead as the Skeet passes over the target tank.

The **CBU-97/B** is the 914lb (415kg) **Sensor-Fused Weapon** currently under development within the context of the Wide-Area Anti-armor Munitions and Assault Breaker programmes to provide US tactical aircraft with the ability to make direct attacks on armoured formations. Each SFW comprises a SUU-64/B Tactical Munitions Dispenser carrying a load of 10

Below:
Internal stowage is still used on long range aircraft such as this Boeing B-52H Stratofortress, allowing the mass carriage of free-fall weapons without too great a drag penalty. The bomb bay can also accommodate the new generation of cluster and dispenser weapons if required, though these are better suited to tactical rather than strategic aircraft. *IMPPS*

Below:
A General Dynamics F-111A shows off its weapons-carriage capability. The white stores are free-fall nuclear weapons (three types), and in the third row of free-fall conventional weapons are 24 dispenser weapons, identifiable by their split casings. *IMPPS*

BLU-108/Bs. When released by the dispenser (under the control of a timer or altitude fuse when the weapon is released from high altitude or in a toss manoeuvre), each of these deploys a parachute to retard and slow its descent to a preset altitude, where a retro-rocket is fired to drive the pack upwards again, spinning rapidly so that the BLU-108/B's four Skeet warheads are articulated outward on levers and then released for individual free-fall, oscillating so that the infra-red sensor can search for a target within an area of about 4,800sq yd (4,015sq m) immediately below it; if no target is detected the Skeet detonates just above the ground to cause blast and fragment damage to any soft-skinned target in the vicinity.

The **Direct Airfield Attack Combined Munition** is under development as an 850lb (385.6kg) weapon based on the SUU-64/B Tactical Munitions Dispenser carrying in its forward section eight BLU-106/B Boosted Kinetic-Energy Penetrator anti-runway bomblets and in its rear section 24 Hunting HB876 area-denial mines. The DAACM is designed for delivery at any speed between 400 and 805mph (644 and 1,295km/hr) and at any altitude between 300 and 40,000ft (90 and 12,190m). The weapon is designed to replace the French Durandal runway-cratering bomb in interim US service, with service entry scheduled for 1990. The BLU-106/Bs are dispensed laterally with varying ejection velocities and retarder-opening delays to create the designed target pattern, and each submunition works in the standard fashion of such weapons, being retarded and then, as soon as the nose of the submunition has dropped to 60-65° below the horizontal, freed from the retarder and accelerated by a solid propellant rocket to penetrate the runway and then to cause considerable crater and heave damage.

Below:
Typical of the latest generation of dispenser weapons is the Avco Direct Airfield Attack Combined Munition: this is based on the US Air Force's Tactical Munitions dispenser and has eight BLU-106/B Boosted Kinetic-Energy Penetrators as its main load for runway cratering, supported by HB876 area-denial minelets to impede repair work. *Avco Systems Division*

'ROCKEYE' CLUSTER BOMB Mk 20 Mod 0

Type: medium anti-tank cluster bomb
Dimensions: diameter 13.2in (0.335m); length 92in (2.337m) without
   fuse cover; fin span 34in (0.864m)
Weight: total round 476lb (215.9kg)
Warhead: 334lb (151.5kg) of bomblets

The **'Rockeye' Cluster Bomb Mk 20 Mod 0** was developed by the US
Naval Weapons Center as an anti-tank cluster bomb for the full range of US
Navy tactical aircraft. The weapon has as its core a Mk 7 Mod 2 dispenser
filled with 247 **Mk 118 Mod 0** anti-tank bomblets. Each of these weighs
1.93lb (0.875kg) and contains a 1.1lb (0.5kg) shaped-charge/fragmentation
warhead with 6.4oz (0.181kg) of explosive. The fragments of the hardened
high-density steel case move at a minimum of 4,000ft (1,219m)/sec, and thus
possess good capability against armoured as well as unarmoured targets.
The nose is fitted with a mechanical time fuse to initiate the charge that splits
the case open and so dispenses the bomblets at a predetermined moment.
The 'Rockeye' can be released at any height down to 250ft (76m) in level
flight or 100ft (30m) in a pitch-up manoeuvre, and the saturation area from a
500ft (150m) release is a 3,333sq yd (2,785sq m) oval. There is also a **Cluster
Bomb Mk 2 Mod 2** which weighs 490lb (222kg).

The **CBU-59/B 'Rockeye II'** is the 766lb (347kg) 'Rockeye' variant for US
Air Force tactical aircraft, and comprises 717 PLU-77/B anti-personnel and
anti-materiel bomblets in a Mk 7 Mod 3 dispenser to create this dual-role
cluster bomb.

The **ISCB-1** was developed on the basis of the 'Rockeye' cluster bomb by
ISC Technologies, the main manufacturer of the 'Rockeye' series, and is the
US forces' latest area-denial cluster weapon. The weapon comprises a Mk 7
dispenser, a Mk 339 nose fuse, a tail cone assembly and a filling of 160
electronically-timed mines plus 65 dummy mines. Up to the time the
bomblets are dispensed the ISCB-1 functions just like the 'Rockeye'.
Thereafter the individual delay of the bomblets is controlled by the
programmable bomb panel located in the tail cone, set before take-off for any
delay between 0sec and 24hr by 10sec increments. This provides area denial
over an area of between 3,600 and 5,625sq yd (3,010 and 4,705sq m).

Above:

This McDonnell Douglas F-15B Eagle carries a prodigious load of 22 'Rockeye' anti-armour cluster bombs; tandem triplets on the centreline, tandem pairs on the tangential hardpoints, and tandem pairs on the inner underwing hardpoints, the last in company with four AIM-9L/M Sidewinder air-to-air missiles. *McDonnell Douglas D4C-120131-4*

Below:

Cutaway sections reveal the loading of the hollow-charge anti-tank bomblets into the dispenser casing of the 'Rockeye II' cluster bomb. The flick-out fins are shown in the extended position. *83-400-514*

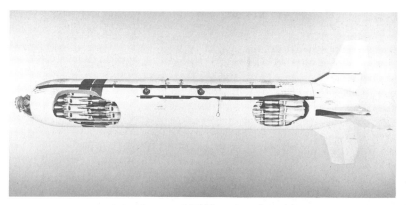